THE MENNONITES

THE MENNONITES

A
*Pictorial History of
Their Lives in
Canada*

ANDREAS SCHROEDER

Douglas & McIntyre
Vancouver/Toronto

Douglas & McIntyre
1615 Venables Street
Vancouver, British Columbia V5L 2H1

Canadian Cataloguing in Publication Data
Schroeder, Andreas, 1946-
    The Mennonites
    ISBN 0-88894-691-0
    1. Mennonites - Canada - History.   I. Title.
FC106.M45S37   1990   289.7′71   C90-091067-4
F1035.M45S37   1990

Editor: Saeko Usukawa
Design by Alexandra Hass
Front jacket photograph by D. Hunsberger
Back jacket photograph courtesy of Louise Schroeder
Frontispiece photograph by George Sawatsky
Typeset by The Typeworks
Printed and bound in Canada by D. W. Friesen & Sons Ltd.

This book is dedicated to Ruth and Roy Vogt—whose quiet generosity, candour and imaginative efforts to put Mennonite principles into practice convinced me more effectively than a dozen books of the efficacy of those principles.

Contents

Preface

Though a great deal of excellent historical research and academic scholarship has been produced about Mennonite history, a great many Mennonites (both religious and ethnic) know their story only in discontinuous fragments. Most of North America's non-Mennonites, of course, know even less. This book is thus intended as a general interest, nonscholarly introduction to the history of one of the world's most singular people.

In writing the text that accompanies the photographs, I have drawn heavily on the works of the late Frank Epp and E. K. Francis. It is my purpose that this book might serve as an introduction to the extensive and authoritative texts these historians have produced.

With respect to the photographs, their collection for a pictorial history of the Mennonites in Canada involved certain difficulties, not the least of which stemmed from the fact that some early Mennonite congregations (pre-World War II) frowned on the taking of photographs and urged or obliged their members to refrain from producing or collecting them. Thus, family photographs other than studio portraits did not become widely available until the 1940s.

Most of the photographs in this book were located in a variety of Mennonite archives throughout the country. Such photographs are often donated to an archive after the death of their owner, making them, if unidentified, difficult or impossible to identify retroactively. Where such photographs were selected for this book, they are identified only by the archive that now owns them.

I wish to express my sincere gratitude to Eugene Derksen of Derksen Printers (Carillon News Archives), Abe Warkentin (editor, *Mennonitische Post*), Ken Reddig (archivist, Mennonite Brethren Bible College), Lawrence Klippenstein and Jim Suderman (archivists, Mennonite Heritage Centre) and Sam Steiner (archivist, Conrad Grebel College) for their exceedingly generous assistance. I have never encountered more helpful, less bureaucratic Keepers of the Photographs.

Andreas Schroeder
Mission, B.C.
1990

Photograph Credits

All photographs are credited in the captions. Some institutions are identifed by their initials:

CMBSC: Centre for Mennonite Brethren Studies in Canada, Winnipeg, Manitoba
MHC: Mennonite Heritage Centre, Winnipeg, Manitoba
CGC: Conrad Grebel College, University of Waterloo, Waterloo, Ontario

The Beginnings of a Singular People

Unwanted Fame

For sheer epic drama—across four and a half centuries, five continents, over forty countries; following or fleeing vicious persecution, utopian enticements, breached promises, perfidious governments, their own prophets—few histories can match the story of the Mennonite people.

And yet, in an irony at least as extraordinary, no people have wanted such attention less. Right from their Anabaptist beginnings in sixteenth-century Europe (Switzerland, Germany, Austria, Holland), the Mennonites wanted only to be left in peace, to live a simple life resolutely "separated" from the world—a world they considered in any case merely transitory, a proving ground to determine their preparedness for God's Kingdom. They wanted nothing to do with the world's wars, its politics, the invariably destructive ambitions of its ecclesiastical and secular leaders and institutions. They wanted simply to follow Christ.

Not surprisingly, Europe's emperors and kings in 1525 weren't any more enamoured of this notion than the Romans had been in Christ's time. To them, the Anabaptists ("rebaptizers") were dangerous troublemakers, whose radical ideas about the separation of church and state, nonresistance and adult baptism struck at the very heart of their states' power structure and the existing social order. These people refused to acknowlege secular authority wherever it differed from God's Word. They rejected the idea of resolving differences by military force. They couldn't be bought with political office, or enticed by secular honours.

Church leaders, both Catholic and Protestant, weren't much happier. For the Anabaptists had consulted the newly available Lutheran German-language bible, a bible they could now read for themselves, and in its New Testament they'd discovered a church quite different from the churches of their own time. Christ's church, as described in the gospel of Luke, was made up of *voluntary* believers, adults who *requested* baptism to signify their decision to become disciples—and this church wasn't run by a vast hierarchy of religious officials, many of whom worked hand in glove with the state. It was a far more democratic church, a religious community in which everyone was considered a priest, all bound together by the precepts of Christ's Sermon on the Mount and a spirit of brotherhood and mutual co-operation. This greatly appealed to the Anabaptists, who promptly began to found their own unauthorized churches on exactly those principles.

Fundamental Principles

By 1527 the first basic Confession of Faith had been set down by a large group of Anabaptists in Schleitheim, Switzerland. It called for a simple, nonworldly lifestyle: nonviolent (love your enemies), nonresistant (turn the other cheek), community service–oriented (everyone is his

Menno Simons, 1496–1561 (MHC)

Previous page: *Interior and exterior views of a Mennonite church in the 1880s* (MHC)

brother's keeper), all specifically reflective of Christ's teachings. It emphasized a direct, personal relationship to God, rather than one mediated through a priestly caste, and it rejected ecclesiastical administrative structures requiring the likes of popes or archbishops. It forbade the swearing of all oaths, even civil ones, as well as service in civil government, police or the military.

Since membership in the church was voluntary, and baptism was considered merely the sign of one's commitment to such discipleship, it followed that this decision could hardly be made at birth or as a child. For that reason the Anabaptists insisted on adult baptism, with an adult's appreciation of the privileges and obligations involved. For anyone who failed to live up to those obligations, there was a system of staged reminders leading (in the worst cases) to complete excommunication.

These ideas—especially the rejection of a state church—spread like wildfire, and by 1529 Europe's secular and ecclesiastical leaders were sufficiently alarmed to formally outlaw Anabaptism throughout most of Protestant and all of Catholic Europe. For the next quarter century (and off and on for the next 150 years) the Anabaptists were persecuted, tortured, burned at the stake and hung by Catholics and Protestants alike. But instead of suppressing them, this aggression merely spread their ideas even further, as the Anabaptists scattered in all directions, desperately seeking safe haven.

These were desperate times for the Anabaptist movement. Its leaders were being murdered almost as fast as they could be elected. Its adherents were too new, too scattered and too independent-minded to permit easy integration. Eventually, the greatest organizational and theological unity was achieved by a former Dutch Catholic priest named Menno Simons, who had become converted to Anabaptism in 1536. Simons soon accepted ordination as an Anabaptist minister, and by 1542 was already sufficiently prominent as a promoter of his new faith that Charles V (Emperor of the Holy Roman Empire) saw fit to put a bounty of 100 guilders—a Catholic priest's annual salary—on his head.

Charles's plan did not succeed. In fact, Simons became so clever at eluding his pursuers' clutches that he was able to remain free for the following nineteen years (eventually dying a natural death in 1561). He proved a tremendously energetic and effective organizer, proselytizing everywhere, visiting scattered Anabaptist groups and writing many of the movement's most seminal treatises. In doing so he redirected some of the Anabaptists' thinking, promoting in particular the principles of nonaggression and nonresistance in marked preference to civil disobedience. He was convinced that the Kingdom of God on earth could not be brought about by "unrighteous means," which for him included such tactics as overthrowing civil governments. So his followers, the "Mennonites," became known primarily as pacifists, and eventually even Anabaptist congregations with no direct connection to Menno Simons became known by the label "Mennonite." Since then, in fact, "Mennonite" has become a widely used generic term for all evangelical Anabaptists.

Safe Havens

Fortunately for the Mennonites of the sixteenth century, not all of Europe's kings and nobles shared the emperor's paranoia about Menno Simons's largely peasant following. Poland's Sigismund II, for example, needed reliable farmers for his land reclamation projects in the Vistula-Nogat delta (near the present-day city of Gdansk), and he wasn't overly fussy about their religious preferences. Word spread quickly, and the steady stream of Mennonite refugees who fled there from northern Germany and Holland proved excellent farmers, quickly developing invaluable expertise in the draining and dyking of marshy, low-lying lands. In return, Sigismund extended special privileges to the Mennonites, guaranteeing them the right of religious worship, their own schools and their own form of baptism. This concentration of Mennonites (whose descendants would eventually settle the Canadian prairies from 1874 onwards) became known as the "Dutch/North German Mennonites," or simply the "Dutch-German Mennonites." By 1600 their prosperous villages dotted the countryside around Danzig, Koenigsberg and Elbing.

Mennonites fleeing persecution in Switzerland and southern Germany also escaped in an easterly direction, finding refuge and work on the estates of sympathetic nobles in Moravia and Bohemia. This group (whose descendants would eventually settle in southern Ontario— then called Upper Canada—in 1786) became known as the "Swiss/South German," or simply "Swiss-German Mennonites," and, like their Dutch-German counterparts, soon enjoyed a reputation as extremely hard-working and inventive farmers. They were the first to introduce such now-common practices as crop rotation, the use of animal manure and lime as fertilizers, and the planting of legumes to add nitrogen to the soil. They were also the first Mennonites to emigrate to North America, in response to an invitation from the famous Quaker William Penn.

Penn had received, in payment of a debt, a large land grant on the North American continent from the English monarch Charles II. Ever an idealist, he had decided to turn this land into a "place of righteous government among men, and a place of civil liberty for the oppressed"—specifically, of course, for his persecuted religious brethren, the Quakers of England, but also for other religious nonconformists such as the Mennonites. (His colony eventually became the state of Pennsylvania.)

Not surprisingly, whole boatloads of religious dissenters poured into the Colony of Penn— including some 100,000 Germans. Over 3,000 of these were Swiss-German Mennonites who arrived between 1710 and 1756, as well as 300 Amish, the followers of an Alsace-based conservative evangelical Anabaptist named Jacob Ammann. Ammann, who believed that strict social discipline was needed to ensure an adequate "separation from the world," insisted on

Mr. and Mrs. J. Zavitz in the 1870s (CGC ARCHIVES)

Facing page: *Toman family, 1880* (CGC ARCHIVES)

such distinctions as beards for the men and bonnets for the women, as well as a rigorous use of the "ban" (excommunication) for dissenters.

All these Mennonites thrived in Pennsylvania. For the first time in their history, they were living under a civic authority that represented a world view virtually identical to their own. The Quaker state was opposed to war and violence, and didn't require the swearing of judicial oaths either. There was plenty of good farmland to be had, and all the religious freedom the Mennonites could probably ever hope to enjoy. Not least, they were surrounded by their own countrymen, with whom they shared a common dialect and many customs. Over time, in fact, this Germanic dialect and culture became known as "Pennsylvania Deutsch," today widely misnamed "Pennsylvania Dutch."

Storm Clouds: Emigrations

What happened next would become a distressingly familiar ordeal for the Mennonites throughout their history. No sooner had they established prosperous and peaceful villages in a safe haven than the spectre of war and the military draft appeared on their horizon once more. In an intriguing (though entirely coincidental) parallel, both the Swiss-German and the Dutch-German Mennonites became confronted by this spectre again at about the same time: the end of the eighteenth century.

In Prussia, which had meanwhile come under Germanic rule, Frederick II was trying to make a name for himself by sparring with half of western Europe. He found the idea of a fast-growing community of pacifists within his borders increasingly unacceptable. In Pennsylvania on the other hand, a growing anti-British sentiment that would soon culminate in the American Revolution deposed the Quaker administration in 1756, and confronted the Mennonites with the requirement to swear a new oath of allegiance. On both continents, the hounds of war were snapping at the Mennonites' heels again.

The solution in both cases also followed a precedent that would become very familiar to the Mennonites over the next two centuries.

In eastern Europe, Tsarina Catherine the Great of Russia, who had heard of the Mennonites' reputation as excellent pioneers and farmers, invited them to settle and develop several large tracts of land along the Dnieper River (in present-day Ukraine) that had been newly liberated from the Turks. In addition to all the usual promises—religious freedom, exemption from the swearing of judicial oaths and from military service, the right to establish and conduct their own schools—she sweetened the pot with an offer of subsidized travel and certain tax concessions.

In North America, following the end of the American Revolution in 1783, the British sovereign offered colonists loyal to the British Crown free land in nearby Canada. Though the

Facing page: *Old Order Mennonites, Waterloo, Ontario* (KITCHENER-WATERLOO RECORD/CGC ARCHIVES)

Mennonites (who hadn't taken sides in the revolution) didn't qualify as Loyalists, the lieutenant-governor of Upper Canada (now Ontario) added a special invitation to them to avail themselves of very inexpensive land there, promising them religious freedom and consideration in the question of military service. Canada too needed dependable pioneers to settle and develop her vast, almost-empty territories.

In both cases, many (but not all) of the Mennonites accepted. They sold their lands and possessions, loaded up their horses and wagons, and trekked many hundreds of miles east or north into a new, uncertain future.

First Mennonite Immigration to Canada

The first Mennonite (Swiss-German) families to arrive in Canada from the United States in 1786 settled in the fertile lowlands between the Niagara escarpment and Lake Ontario. Two years later a second group settled in Welland County, and another in the area that eventually became the city of Hamilton. By 1803 there were twenty-five families in Waterloo county, and thirty-three between Vineland and Beamsville in Lincoln County. But the greatest single boost for Mennonite emigration to Canada at this time occurred after twenty-six enterprising Mennonite farmers joined together to form the German Land Company, which purchased 60,000 acres in Waterloo and 45,195 acres in Woolwich Township for resale to their Mennonite coreligionists in the U.S. This, plus a short but harsh depression in Pennsylvania in the 1820s convinced many more to leave the United States, and by 1841 there were some 5,500 Mennonites scattered throughout thirty townships in Upper Canada.

The Amish came to Upper Canada from both Pennsylvania *and* Europe, after an Amish farmer from Bavaria arrived in Waterloo County in 1822, secured a large land reserve in the county's township of Wilmot, and returned to spread the word among Amish settlements in the Palatinate and Alsace. Amish migration to Canada from both Europe and the U.S. continued for the following fifty years, giving this Mennonite group a secure and widespread base in southwestern Ontario.

Mennonite Settlement Patterns

Since the two major streams of Mennonites—the Swiss-German Mennonites and the Dutch-German Mennonites—were fated to meet in Canada less than half a century later in 1874, a brief comparison of their different colonization/settlement patterns might be useful.

Their differences were considerable. In Russia, the Dutch-German Mennonites had nego-

Mary and Jacob Hallman (mother and son), New Hamburg, Ontario, 1914 (CGC ARCHIVES)

Facing page: *Leah and Rachel Schrag, southern Ontario, 1880* (CGC ARCHIVES)

tiated their colonization agreements as a group, had moved in groups, and had designed their settlements with the co-operative needs of the group in mind. Their overriding purpose had always been to maintain a "separateness" from the surrounding world. So their colonies ended up being virtually autonomous ministates, each with its own administrative infra-structure, taxation system, disciplinary regulations and educational/welfare institutions. Their villages were laid out on a close-habitat/open-field system, in which the houses (typi-cally a house/barn combination) were set out at regular intervals along both sides of a single street, each with a narrow strip of land behind for a farmyard or garden. In addition, each family received its own parcel of land for individual cultivation elsewhere within the colony's boundaries, plus access to communally held pastureland. This kind of settlement design vir-tually assured "separateness," not to mention communal togetherness and economic self-sufficiency.

The Swiss-German Mennonites in Upper Canada were in no position to develop this kind of sectarian settlement. For one thing, they had emigrated to Canada not as entire villages or congregations but mostly as single or extended families. They settled in Ontario in the same way, as families or in small groups at best. Even when they bought land from the large tracts of the German Land Company, these lots were broken up by the fourteen out of every forty-eight lots (interspersed, not contiguous) that were reserved, by the Constitutional Act of 1791, for the Crown and the Anglican state church. An 1819 petition to the lieutenant-governor by the Mennonites in Lincoln County, requesting that an undivided block of land be set aside specifically for Mennonites in several new, as yet unsurveyed townships, was denied.

Even in those settlements where their large numbers gave them a statistical majority (Woolwich, Waterloo), the Swiss-German Mennonites didn't form closed communities in the "Russian" sense. For one thing, they weren't as obviously different from their neighbours as were the Dutch-German Mennonites from the seminomadic tribes who lived around them in the Ukraine. For another, the traditions they'd developed in the United States hadn't gen-erally stressed that much religious *and* civic unity.

So if, despite all the above, the Swiss-German Mennonites did develop informally cohesive groups and even Mennonite-specific settlements throughout southern Ontario, it was prob-ably more because of sheer family size and congregational growth. Mennonite families on both sides of the Atlantic were justly famous for their size. Six to eight children represented the norm rather than the exception, and reports of twelve to sixteen raised few eyebrows. In-termarriage at such a birth rate quickly created prodigious family trees. So this—plus the fact that their young men tended to stick to farming, preferably not too far from the ancestral home—created large well-bonded communities even where they weren't visibly formalized by statute or incorporation.

Jacob Shantz, Kitchener, Ontario, 1895
(CGC ARCHIVES)

William Hembling, deacon, 1858 (CGC ARCHIVES)

Right: *The J. Y. Shantz family, circa 1900* (MHC)

The Mennonite Community

A Farming People

As a people, the Mennonites were at this time primarily farmers, though a small percentage—in Upper Canada probably no more than 5 per cent—worked in such trades as sawmilling, gristmilling, blacksmithing and stonemasonry. (In Prussia, where land hadn't been as easy to acquire, a somewhat larger percentage had become cartwrights, cobblers, tailors, tanners and brewers.) In fact, for at least another 175 years, farming for the Mennonites would remain almost a calling—a vocation designated by God as the one most right and proper for a Mennonite to pursue. Many felt (and some said) that a mere businessman would probably find it as difficult to be a good Mennonite as a camel to pass through the eye of a needle.

The Mennonite Family

The family—its cohesion and its spiritual health—stood at the core of Mennonite life. At its centre stood the church—the larger family. "Worldly" influences were resolutely kept out of both, including such entertainments as dancing, secular concerts or the like. These could only be dangerous distractions from a Mennonite's singular purpose: to lead a simple, Christlike life, at the end of which Salvation awaited. To keep distractions at bay, the day-to-day emphasis was kept on hard work—not difficult to justify in any case, when it took that and more to wrest a living from frontier land.

Both family and church were solidly patriarchal. The man was the undisputed head of his household. Only men could be elected or designated as church Elders, ministers or officials.

The farm work was also generally segregated. The men and boys worked with the horses, logging, clearing, ploughing and seeding the land. Most men also learned the basics of working with leather, stone/bricks, wood and sometimes metal. The girls and women cared for the house and the animals, milked the cows, cooked the meals, planted vegetable and flower gardens, and learned to weave, spin and sew. Everyone joined forces at harvest time. The Mennonites were famous for simple but bountiful meals, and their cellars were usually filled with vegetables and preserves. They also enjoyed a well-deserved reputation for splendid pies and cakes.

For all their hard work and modest lifestyle, the Mennonites were a gregarious people. This was particularly evident on Sunday afternoons after church, when much back-and-forth visiting was not only permitted but encouraged. They placed a great deal of importance on kinship ties and their family trees; the weddings, funerals and gatherings of relatives as far removed as the fourth rank were all attended as eagerly as those of their own immediate fam-

Mennonite families in Rosenbach, Manitoba, 1919 (MHC)

Previous page: *A Mennonite woman* (GEORGE SAWATSKY)

ily. Given their large families, this made the concept of a boring Sunday afternoon virtually incomprehensible.

Such gatherings, of course, served many important functions. They maintained strong family and community cohesion. They offset the sterner side of a demanding religious lifestyle. They kept everyone up-to-date on the news. And last but not least, they provided courtship opportunities for the young.

At this stage in Mennonite history, virtually all phases of a courtship occurred under adult supervision. Young people saw and met each other either at church or at family gatherings. Clandestine messages were exchanged through the medium of brothers and sisters. By the time anything as public as a formal visit between a young man and a young woman occurred, a committment to marriage was as good as confirmed. Engagements were either announced from the pulpit or banns were published in the European tradition.

Given such a tradition, it's hardly surprising that intermarriage between Mennonites and non-Mennonites was extremely rare. It was even fairly unusual for Mennonites of different conference affiliations to intermarry. And once married, only adultery was considered a legitimate reason for divorce. Since they stressed the spiritual nature of the marriage bond—in which one's obligations lay primarily with Christ—they expected that bond to be permanent. The rate of divorce among Mennonites was therefore almost zero.

Mary Nahrgang, Lillian Snyder and Nancy Snyder, 1902 (CGC ARCHIVES)

Land Ownership

Though their religious principles and social system stressed a co-operative and fraternal lifestyle, the Mennonite Anabaptists never did subscribe to a practical communism, as did some other Anabaptist sects such as the Hutterites. The Mennonites always owned their houses, land and personal property as individuals rather than as a group, and thus held each other individually responsible for both possessions and debts. Of the few exceptions to this general rule, the most notable was probably the land owned by the Dutch-German colonies in Russia; though much of this land was divided into individually owned plots, some pastureland was held in common and was administered by the colonies' leaders for the general good. And their Anabaptist traditions obviously made many of them readily amenable to the idea of co-operatives and similar economic unions (such as those which sprang up across the Canadian prairies during the Depression). But basically, most Mennonite enterprises remained individualistic and voluntary.

The Hunsberger family, Maple Grove, Ontario, 1918 (CGC ARCHIVES)

Mutual Aid

If strong religious convictions and large families constituted the cornerstones of a strong
Mennonite community, then its traditions of communal self-sufficiency and mutual aid were
certainly ingredients in the mortar. Both the Swiss-German and the Dutch-German Mennonites independently developed almost identical traditions of this kind. Both groups, for example, developed variations on the "working bee," in which groups or whole communities
join together to accomplish swiftly and efficiently what most individuals wouldn't have been
capable of managing as readily on their own: building houses, barns, roads, schools and
meeting houses, as well as mass harvesting the community's crops.

Following the same logic, and linking it with a sensible frugality, the Mennonites also
created their own damage insurance plan (fire, hail, storm)—the first in North America being
the Ontario Mennonite Aid Union, established in 1866. This sort of insurance had the virtue
of being inexpensive (since it was nonprofit) and of keeping the premiums "in-house." The
Dutch-German Mennonites in Russia not only instituted their own damage insurance, but
added a "Waisenamt" (Orphans' Bureau), an early form of welfare programme which assumed the care of orphans and widows and protected their interests in estate or inheritance
matters. The Waisenamt, in fact, became a de facto credit union, a "bank with a heart," bor-
rowing and lending money within a closed Mennonite community for the benefit of all.

Schooling

About schooling, the two groups shared similar views but dissimilar arrangements. Both
considered religious instruction for their children of enormous importance, and any government which tried to curb this objective was always met with strong resistance. Furthermore,
both groups used High German as their language of religious instruction, so that the teaching
of German was also considered, at least at this stage in their history, a non-negotiable issue.

Fortunately for the Dutch-German Mennonites in Russia, all this had been negotiated
prior to their emigration there, and until the Russian Revolution in 1917, the Tsarist governments maintained a benign, hands-off policy with respect to Mennonite schools—which were
paid for, operated by and restricted to the Mennonites themselves.

The Swiss-German Mennonites of Upper Canada hadn't managed to negotiate any special arrangements regarding schools, but for the first fifty years this wasn't a problem, since
there was no government-funded or government-controlled school system in existence anyway. All schooling was by individual initiative, and the Mennonites took full advantage of
this. Their various ad hoc community schools used German as the language of instruction

Top and bottom: *Barn raising,
Waterloo, Ontario* (CGC ARCHIVES)

Facing page: *Hugo Bartel and oxen,
1907* (MHC)

and taught religion, reading, writing and arithmetic. School terms were restricted to the winter months, and for teachers they used virtually anyone they could find—anyone who wasn't suited to farming and/or hadn't the usual farming responsibilities. Such schooling arrangements continued until 1842, when the first Common Schools Act was passed.

When it came to religious instruction, one of the main pedagogical devices used by both Swiss-German and Dutch-German Mennonites was the Catechism. A question-and-answer summary of Christian doctrine, the Catechism had been used in early Christian times and then readopted by the Anabaptists. The successful study and memorization of the Catechism was usually followed by baptism and formal induction as a member of the congregation. Though baptism was technically strictly faith-related, unduly early baptism was frowned upon (since church membership required a voluntary, mature decision), and most young people waited until they were of marriage age (sixteen to twenty) before formally joining the church.

Mennonite school children in Saskatchewan, 1904 (CMBSC ARCHIVES)

Church Services

Until the turn of the nineteenth century, church services among the Mennonites in Ontario were much the same as Mennonite church services the world over. In pioneering days, when congregations were small, people gathered for Sunday morning services in someone's home. As the congregations grew, modest meeting houses were built. Services were generally around two hours long, and they were solemn, dignified affairs. They began with the singing of several hymns, often led by a chorister, followed by a short introductory opening delivered by a junior minister. The congregation then knelt in silent prayer. The senior minister or Elder then delivered the main sermon, a good part of which was often read from a collection of published sermons. At the conclusion, other ministers or worthies rose briefly to attest to the legitimacy of what had been preached. Occasionally they even added a few thoughts of their own. The Elder then concluded the service with an audible prayer, following the closing hymn with the benediction.

At this time Mennonite church services were straightforward and unadorned. The men sat on one side of the church, the women on the other. There were no Sunday schools, no instruments to accompany the congregation's singing, no church choirs. Fire and brimstone preaching was considered in poor taste among the Mennonite leadership. The hymns were long and slow-paced, and were sung in unison. Like noisy preaching, four-part harmony singing was considered too splashy. For several centuries the chief source of Mennonite hymns was the *Ausbund*, a collection of hymns about the martyred heroes of the Anabaptist faith, though by 1836 many congregations—both Canadian and American—were using a collection assembled by Elder Benjamin Eby of Waterloo. Eby's hymns were shorter and paced a little faster, though still, by today's standards, quite solemn.

John Funk, 1900 (MHC)

Clerical Functions

Though the Anabaptists subscribed to the principle that "everyone was a priest," it only made common sense to choose specific people for specific clerical functions, such as the offices of deacon, minister and/or Elder. These were all still lay functions, performed by men without any special theological training. The positions were restricted to Mennonite males, who contributed their time without pay and performed their duties in addition to their regular farm work. The choice among nominees was often decided by lot (for example, having nominees choose among a pile of hymnals, one of which contained the fateful slip of paper), followed by ordination. Ordination was generally for life.

Mennonite congregations usually grew by division. When a congregation became too

Previous page: *A gathering of Mennonite women* (CMBSC ARCHIVES)

large it divided, using the existing church's resources to finance the establishment of the satellite congregation. In such cases, the Elder of the existing church often assisted in the nomination and ordination of a new Elder, minister or deacon for the satellite group. The clergy was almost always chosen from among the congregation's own members.

The "Anabaptist Sickness"

Being chosen an Elder in the Mennonite Church could prove a good deal more hectic and difficult than one might expect from a people dedicated to peace, brotherly love and the simple emulation of Christ. The reason for this involved one of the Anabaptists' most celebrated and liberalizing principles—the insistence that every Christian be permitted his or her own interpretation of God's word or will. In short order this proved to be the source of both the movement's greatest spiritual strength and its greatest organizational weakness. Already at the very beginning, when representatives of the widely scattered Anabaptist groups had met in both Germany and Switzerland to try to synchronize their religious views, this principle had shown its capacity for promoting or at least permitting a great deal of splintering and fractiousness. This tended to happen so readily that it became known by the movement's enemies as the "Taeuferkrankheit" (Anabaptist Sickness). Though Menno Simons had managed, through his strong emphasis on peace, mediation and discipleship, to manoeuvre this "disease" into a temporary remission, its relentless, cyclical reappearance was to prove a monumental headache for the Mennonites in the centuries to come.

Upheaval in the Church

As the nineteenth century progressed in North America, symptoms of the Anabaptist Sickness began to appear once again in Mennonite congregations on both sides of the border. Its causes were many and diverse. Historically, of course, frequent persecution, many migrations, and changing settlement patterns had fostered all kinds of fragmentation again and again. Personality clashes among Mennonite leaders certainly contributed to the problem as well. More recently, the American Revolution had reactivated a general public zeal for popular democracy, and while the Mennonites weren't directly affected, it couldn't help but put into a more negative light the autocratic rule of many of their Elders, who had become accustomed (particularly in trying times) to leading their flocks without much consultation or flexibility. In an effort to shield their congregations from the pernicious influences of the surrounding world, they sometimes fell back on overly legalistic interpretations of church rules and traditions, and the power of the ban was sometimes used too readily to silence dissenters.

On the other hand, those inclined to be more orthodox complained that the churches had become too permissive. They accused church leaders of having turned a blind eye to members' attendance at county fairs and horse races—not to mention voting in government elections. They demanded stricter discipline and a more rigorous use of the ban. Arguments about the precise definition of such concepts as "worldly," "spiritual sloth" and "nonresistance" became more heated.

Any time that progressives and conservatives got into an argument about religion, the matter of dress was sure to come up. Some Elders insisted on a prayer veil for women and the traditional plain-coat for men as a virtual church uniform. In some churches, rebellious members were refused communion or even banned for refusing to wear them. Wearing a tie (vanity) could provoke an uproar. To use or not to use oil-cloth coverings for wagons (modernism) became for some congregations a major theological issue. In all such cases, however, it was rarely the actual item of contention that lay at the heart of the argument, but rather the fear of the thin edge of the wedge; the not unfounded worry that once the door had been opened for small changes, large ones (and "the World" from which the Mennonites had always tried to keep themselves separate) would be sure to follow.

Revivalism

As if that weren't enough, by the 1840s a Methodist-style revivalism had begun to sweep North America's Protestant churches, and in time breached even the most "separated" Mennonite congregations. Many Mennonites became caught up in its religious fervour. Such pulpit-thumping hellfire sermons were unknown in Mennonite churches, and while many resisted them, others became enthralled. They became intrigued by the Methodists' use of Sunday schools, church choirs, musical instruments in church, weekday prayer meetings, full-immersion baptism and missionary outreach initiatives. These struck them as revitalizing and progressive. Others saw them as a tidal wave of distracting, dangerous and even worldly religious trappings.

Under such pressures, people reacted variously. Some instinctively drew back—barricading themselves behind an insistent, almost desperate conservatism. Others pushed ahead, riding a progressive wave until their own limits had been reached. Naturally, these limits varied widely. Some wanted to free themselves almost entirely from the old traditions. Others wanted more religious progress, but not at the expense of the old traditions. Still others wanted to keep a few of the traditions, but not those that conflicted with a greater emphasis on revivalism and missionary outreach.

Old Order Amish, Waterloo, Ontario
(D. HUNSBERGER/CGC ARCHIVES)

New Alliances

Many Elders and ministers began to find themselves out of step with their congregations. In the agonizing that followed, it was sometimes hard to distinguish between genuine theological arguments and mere personality clashes, between genuine reformers and mere opportunists. Many congregations eventually split, and some split several times. New alliances were formed; some held, some didn't. A few groups or congregations abandoned the Mennonite fold altogether.

This too was to become an all too common phenomenon among Mennonite congregations the world over—and nowhere more than in North America, where it would happen again and again. And while the names and places differed, the pattern repeated itself often enough that it may be useful to examine it in greater detail here, then apply it as a useful paradigm later.

One thing that must be kept in mind about the Mennonites is that their "Anabaptist Sickness" was mostly a direct result of their religious principles, not their spleen. Ironically, though everyone speaks yearningly about peace, the people most likely to be shot by both enemies and friends have always been the pacifists. Furthermore, no society really likes outsiders. And traditional Mennonites have always been both. This means that they've always been under tremendous pressure by any society in which they've lived to become integrated, assimilated, nondifferent—to stop being Mennonites. And the success of that effort has always been a traditional Mennonite's greatest fear. That's because its success would take them right back to 1525, when it all began. That's why they had rebelled against the assimilated state churches of Europe—in the Anabaptists' view, these churches had become hopelessly compromised and corrupted by the temptations of "the World." A traditional Mennonite has had little faith that such temptations could be successfully resisted by most individuals, let alone churches, once the door has been pried open.

So virtually every argument within the Mennonite churches has always led back, directly or indirectly, to the question of "separateness." About how separate one should (must) be. About what separateness even means. About whether this dress, that car or the use of this or that language has or will compromise a member's (or church's) sacred separateness.

Cressman Mennonite meeting house, Breslau, Ontario, 1907 (CGC ARCHIVES)

The "New" Mennonites

The irreconcilability of just such arguments had, by the 1870s, seen two major alliances of "progressive" congregations (who called themselves the "New" Mennonites) break away from the main group of Mennonite churches in Ontario: the General Conference Mennonite Churches of North America, and the Mennonite Brethren in Christ Church. And in reaction

A Mennonite church in Duchess, Alberta, 1950 (CGC ARCHIVES)

to this progressiveness, a number of smaller, very conservative alliances soon broke away in the opposite direction. These included the Church of God in Christ Mennonite, the Old Order Mennonites, and the Reformed Mennonites.

Trying to summarize the principles around which these breakaway groups were formed is fraught with peril, since they shared many of the same concerns and often differed only in emphasis or method. However, some distinctions can be made.

The most aggressively "progressive" group, the Mennonite Brethren in Christ were strongly influenced by the Methodists. Their ministers preached with great zeal. Open-air revival meetings were common, with four-part singing and instrumental accompaniment. Religious conversion (new birth) and personal piety were considered absolutely essential. A great emphasis was put on missionary outreach work, de-emphasizing the traditional Mennonite insistence on nonconformity, nonresistance and any other obvious differences between Mennonites and non-Mennonite Protestants. Mennonite Brethren in Christ churches also took most readily to the use of the English language for church services. On the other hand, they tended to be quite rigid in their opposition to drinking, smoking, unbecoming dress and worldly amusements, many of which they considered excommunication offences. Their churches were administered by powerful superintendents and were tightly organized, stressing obedience rather than democracy.

The General Conference Mennonite churches, though also progressive, had chosen a more moderate approach and were less inclined to jettison Mennonite distinctions. The conference was made up of a fairly wide range of churches, loosely unified under the motto: "In fundamentals unity, in secondary matters diversity, in all things charity." It was democratic to a fault; overall conference decisions were only binding on those churches which decided to accept the decisions, and in general member congregations were administered by elected church boards rather than by an Elder. They shared an enthusiasm with the Mennonite Brethren for Sunday schools, weekday prayer meetings, four-part singing and instrumental accompaniment, but tended to be more liberal and intellectual in their perception of evangelistic issues. Rather than a rigid set of rules about personal behaviour, the General Conference merely frowned on worldly amusements, voting, drinking and unbecoming dress, and stressed charity in judging one another on these matters.

Conservative Mennonites

The conservative and ultraconservative groups soon found themselves in a comparatively thankless defensive position, mostly reacting against what they saw as the excesses of the progressive groups' initiatives. They shook their heads at all this sudden preoccupation with constitutions, committee meetings, programmes, statistics, reports and a welter of evening religious meetings. None of this had been necessary before; what was wrong with simply living your faith quietly, and tilling the land as God had intended you to do? They foresaw, or at least intuited, the fact that many new technological innovations would turn out to be people's masters rather than their servants, and this too they perceived as ultimately danger-ous or damaging to the Mennonites' traditional values. Most seriously, they worried that the progressive emphasis on personal salvation, personal ethics and personal evangelism would break down their traditional fraternal, cohesive religious community.

Under all this pressure, their response to this newness tended toward an ever-increasing, often extremely legalistic insistence on the rigid maintaining of the old rules and regulations. Minor issues, under such circumstances, were invariably judged by their major implications, and this led to an increasingly negative attitude. The use of brass buckles, buttons, or jewel-lery of any kind could land a member in a great deal of trouble. The same applied to furnish-ings. Homes were left largely unadorned; no curtains, pictures or wallpaper. Education beyond a basic learning of the three Rs was considered "prideful," unnecessary and danger-ous. Many "Old Order" (as they came to be known) Mennonite groups thus defined them-selves not so much by what they were as by what they *were not*—by what they did not do, did not permit and did not believe.

Christian and Mary Gascho, Zurich, Ontario, 1911 (CGC ARCHIVES)

And in the Middle . . .

Pummelled in this way on all sides, the remaining mainstream churches (confusingly called "Old" Mennonites to distinguish them from both the progressive New Mennonites and the ultraconservative Old Order Mennonites) did what every group in the middle always does— they went, very slowly, in both directions at once. They adopted some of the progressives' church service innovations, but took firmer stands against moustaches, photography, and at-tendance at country or city fairs, exhibitions or commercial amusements. Membership in unions was prohibited; nonpayment of debts could result in excommunication. Yet they did officially recognize the use of both languages (German and English) as legitimate for church use and supported the idea of a missionary movement.

The Amish

The generally more conservative Amish, though somewhat slower in responding to all these developments, were in the end unable to avoid them and followed much the same pattern.

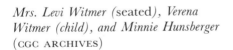

Mrs. Levi Witmer (seated), *Verena Witmer (child), and Minnie Hunsberger* (CGC ARCHIVES)

They split in three directions:

1) the progressive Amish (also known as "Church-Amish," because they permitted the construction of dedicated meeting houses);

2) the "mainstream" Amish (confusingly self-styled as "Conservative" Amish, to point up their difference from the

3) ultraconservative Old Order Amish (also known as "House-Amish," because they refused to permit the construction of meeting houses or churches).

Roughly speaking, the clerical configuration of most Mennonite churches tended to mirror their ecclesiastical orientation. In other words, the more conservative congregations tended to be "Elder-based"—single congregations both led and administered by a strong, patriarchal Elder who was elected for life. The progressives, on the other hand, belonged to an alliance (conference) of like-minded congregations organized on a regional or continental basis. While they too were led in spiritual matters by an Elder and (often) a group of lay ministers and deacons, their congregations were generally administered by elected church boards or committees.

All this having been said, it remains true that ordering the many Mennonite schisms and divisions into three neat rows makes both the process and the result seem far too tidy and contained. It was, and continues to be, much less clearly defined than that, not least because the different groups could often not even agree among themselves on where they stood. Conservatism and progress are always matters of degree, and every congregation mixed these elements in varying combinations.

Parallel Developments in Russia

Though an ocean and thousands of miles separated the Mennonites of North America and Russia, a remarkably similar restlessness began to trouble the colonies in Russia in the early nineteenth century. In founding these colonies, like their coreligionists in North America, the Mennonites had been searching for utopia. In both cases, in a comparatively short time—and in economic terms at least—they'd come as close to finding it as they could reasonably have expected. But like their coreligionists in North America, they seemed to be finding their spiritual utopia receding with every economic success. In the Russian colonies too, complaints grew louder about rampant materialism, a lax spiritual discipline, knee-jerk religiosity and too much worldliness. By the 1820s these colonies experienced the establishment (against vigorous Elder resistance) of its first breakaway congregation—the "Kleine Gemeinde" (Little Congregation), led by ultraconservative reformer Klaas Reimer. Reimer thundered

Old Order Mennonites in southern Ontario (D. HUNSBERGER/CGC ARCHIVES)

against everything from card-playing to the wearing of moustaches, and eventually led his small flock to found a new colony of their own.

By the 1860s, the strong revivalist influences of European pietism and the British & Foreign Bible Society had breached the Russian Mennonites' "separateness" as well, finding an enthusiastic response from both reform-minded adults and many increasingly disaffected young people. For the latter in particular, "calcified" church services had become boring, and many flocked to hear the rousing sermons of a visiting Lutheran evangelist. This led to what became known as "Die Froehliche Richtung" (The Exuberance Movement), and soon resulted in a second, much larger breakaway group, who called themselves (once more in uncanny parallel) the "Mennonite Brethren." This group, in fact, was fated through emigration and aggressive proselytizing to become, eventually, the second largest conference in Canada.

The J. P. Peters family (father deceased) just before leaving Russia for Canada, 1920 (KATHY PETERS)

Susanna (Wiens) and David P. Goerzen, and their son, David, who settled in Crossfield, Alberta, 1927 (KATHY PETERS)

Broken Promises

The ill wind that finally fanned the various discontents in the Mennonite Russian colonies into open flame was the age-old issue of military service. Russia had just lost the Crimean War (1854–56) and was being threatened by Bismarck and his newly constituted Germany. Alarmed, Tsar Alexander II called for a country-wide conscription in 1870, and despite earlier promises to the contrary, informed religious nonconformists that they would have to cooperate or leave Russia. At the same time, the Mennonites were informed that henceforth Russian would replace German as the official language of instruction at all their (formerly private) Mennonite schools.

The alarm bells that promptly began ringing throughout the Mennonite colonies were heard as far away as Canada and the United States, both of which had been expanding westward across their respective portions of North America, and now needed large numbers of agricultural pioneers to settle the vast western plains. In Canada's case this was particularly urgent, since its leaders feared an American inclination to annex the Canadian prairies and needed a string of Canadian settlements across this territory to fly the Union Jack. Both countries promptly sent agents and promoters into the Mennonite colonies in Russia.

From a strictly agricultural perspective, Canada didn't have a particularly impressive offer to make. The Mennonite delegation that travelled to Manitoba in June of 1873 found the mosquitoes almost intolerable, much of the land swampy, the trails poorly travelled, and access to commercial centres (for the selling of produce) difficult and expensive. The United States, on the other hand, could offer a milder climate and better access to shipping facilities. Both countries offered land grants of approximately 160 acres per male over the age of twenty-one, though the American offer was less than specific about the cost.

But on the issue of exemption from military duty, Canada definitely had the edge. Its Militia Act of 1793 specifically exempted Mennonites from such service, whereas the United States had no such federal law and refused to consider one. It could only point to the fact that there was no compulsory military service in the U.S.A. at that time.

As the competition heated up, the Canadian government attempted to improve its position by adding the following additional enticements:

1) the grant of an entire reserve or block of land (not broken up by grants to railway companies) set aside for the exclusive use of the Mennonites, thus making possible the same kind of compact settlement they had developed in Russia;

2) full exercise of religious principles and education of children without restriction;

3) the right to affirm instead of to swear in taking the oath;

4) transportation credits of up to $30 per adult, for travel from Hamburg to Fort Garry, Manitoba; also, supplies for the sea voyage.

Most of these provisions, in fact, were part of Canada's standard immigration policy, but the right to exclusive block settlement was new—as was the right to educate their own children, a provision actually outside the jurisdiction of the federal government, and one that would cause the Mennonites a great deal of grief in the years to come.

The Russians apparently hadn't believed the Mennonites would emigrate over the military service issue, and when they discovered the threat was real, mounted a major effort to dissuade them from leaving. Russian conscription law was changed to allow for "alternate service" (which for the Mennonites came to mean work in forestry camps). Canadian, British and American settlement agents were refused further permission to visit the colonies. Exit visas became difficult and time-consuming to get. High-level government officials summoned the Mennonite leaders and did their best to convince them to stay.

1874: Emigration

In the end, no one got everything, but everyone got something. About a third of the Mennonites in Russia—some 17,000 of them—decided to emigrate, regardless of Russian promises. By and large, those for whom the religious issues were paramount and non-negotiable—such as military exemption, the right to educate their children as they saw fit, the right to construct their villages in the traditional communal, separatist fashion—chose Canada. The rest chose the United States.

The trip from Russia to Manitoba took up to eight weeks. Since Russia refused to allow immigrants to leave via Russian seaports, the Mennonites had to trek to Odessa, travel on to Hamburg by rail, spend three weeks crossing the Atlantic, continue by train from Quebec or Montreal to Toronto, travel overland to Collingwood, by boat to Duluth (Minnesota), overland to Moorehead (Minnesota), and finally up the Red River back into Canada and on to St. Agathe, Manitoba. Not the least of the many bewildering afflictions they had to contend with along the way was predatory American agents attempting to woo them, even at this late stage, away from Canada and on to Kansas. From an economic standpoint alone, such efforts were understandable, for these immigrants were not the usual destitute pioneers. The value of their immediate contribution to Manitoba's wealth, conservatively estimated, exceeded $1,000,000.

When this emigration had finally run its course (1874–80), approximately 7,500 Mennonites had uprooted themselves from Russia to the plains of southern Manitoba. They consisted for the most part of entire colonies, including most of Klaas Reimer's ultraconservative Kleine Gemeinde from the Borozenko Colony, as well as the Bergthal and Fuerstenland colonies. These were joined by some hundreds of Prussian Mennonites from the Vistula

A typical Mennonite house and barn combination, this one in southeast Manitoba (CARILLON NEWS ARCHIVES)

Mennonites arriving in Manitoba, 1874
(MHC)

delta, and several groups of Ontario Mennonites, who also seized the opportunity for a new start for either religious or economic reasons. To assist everyone, particularly the new immigrants, the Mennonites of Ontario established the Russian Aid Committee, which raised about $100,000 in resettlement aid.

And so the two main streams of Mennonites in the world—the Swiss-German Mennonites and the Dutch-German Mennonites—had finally linked up in the New World.

First Mennonites in Manitoba

The first disappointment in store for the initial wave of Russian Mennonites to arrive in Manitoba in 1874 was the fact that the land set aside for them on the east side of the Red River was of very poor quality. Its timber was meagre and the soil was poor; some areas were largely sand and gravel, others cluttered with stones and boulders. Several large sections were mostly marsh. Charitably, it can only be assumed that agricultural authorities had picked this area (which came to be known as the East Reserve) over far more fertile land nearby because it contained trees and bodies of water, both resources of value to pioneer homesteaders. The vast, treeless (but far more fertile) grasslands farther to the south and west had already defeated earlier, non-Mennonite settlers.

But what Canadian authorities hadn't considered was the fact that these Mennonites, with their 150-year history on the Russian steppes, were entirely at home in vast, treeless country. So they applied for a reserve on just such country west of the Red River, well south and west of the first reserve. It came to be known as the West Reserve. Subsequent waves of Mennonite immigrants settled there instead, as well as some 400 families who abandoned their East Reserve homesteads after much wasted effort. Since not *all* the land in the East Reserve was hopeless, however, approximately 400 of the first immigrant families remained there and, over time, used trial and error to learn how to coax a reasonable living from it.

Unfortunately, the first two crop years in both reserves were almost total failures. Grasshoppers were the cause in 1875, and early frosts killed the wheat in 1876. The settlers had to draw heavily on $260,000 in loans that the Russian Aid Committee had negotiated from the federal government, loans guaranteed in varying amounts by many Ontario Mennonites. It was an early and critically important instance of Mennonites helping other, distant Mennonites—an impulse that would be called on with increasing regularity, worldwide, throughout the following century.

The settlers had also brought over with them, intact, their various social institutions such as the Waisenamt, their disaster insurance and even their village administrative structures.

Cutting pulpwood in southern Manitoba, early 1900s (CMBSC ARCHIVES)

Facing page: *Reproduction of an 1870s Mennonite sod hut, Mennonite Heritage Village* (CARILLON NEWS ARCHIVES)

These began to function virtually from the day of the settlers' arrival, and helped enormously to relieve many difficulties and accidents.

In the decades that followed, the hard work began to pay off. It wasn't long before the grain being produced in the more fertile West Reserve exceeded local requirements and was being shipped out for sale. By 1878 they were shipping seven carloads of flax to a Mennonite oil manufacturing concern in Ontario. The East Reserve immigrants, having focussed primarily on subsistence farming, produced a lot of dairy products as cash crops. Cheese factories sprang up, and four grist mills.

By 1886, 70,000 additional acres had been brought under cultivation. Five years later this had risen to 111,000 acres. By 1921 the total acreage under cultivation stood at 242,000.

One of the first tasks the settlers had undertaken after their arrival was the planting of thousands of trees—maple, poplar, cottonwood—both as windbreaks and for decoration. This too was a tradition straight out of the Ukrainian steppes, and it suited their new prairie villages splendidly. The Mennonites had also developed quite a reputation as lovers of flowers, and these were soon blooming in their gardens and flower boxes all over southern Manitoba. They introduced the dahlia to Canada, and within a few years Mennonite villages were renowned far and wide for their colourful beauty. As had been the case in Tsarist Russia, and likewise for the Mennonites of Ontario, their settlements were soon on the itinerary of a steady stream of provincial and federal officials wanting to see this "agricultural miracle."

Mennonite Settlements in Manitoba

Although most Mennonite settlements in those early days in Manitoba tried to maintain the close-habitat/open-field village design of their Russian past, it soon became evident that the *solidaristic* principles on which such a design was based were in fundamental conflict with the *individualistic* principles underlying Canada's Dominion Land Act. The government, as per its immigration promises, may have permitted the Mennonites to settle two large areas of reserved land as a group, but the only way all that land could be registered, according to the regulations of the Land Act, was individually: one quarter section per male over twenty-one, and each quarter section had to be legally registered in the name of that male.

When the Mennonites first discovered they couldn't legally own their land as a group, they simply shrugged, got each man to sign his form, and then ignored the forms. They settled the land in their traditional fashion, assigning each village member a piece of individual property, but holding much additional property in common—the choice of who got what land being determined not by a surveyor's lines but by factors such as the relative quality of the land, its accessibility, proximity to water, and so on. In their solidaristic system, an effort was made to give every member an equal share of roughly similar qualities of land—a determination no

surveyor could be the least bit interested in.

From the perspective of a Dominion Lands Office, of course, the design of the Mennonite villages meant that everybody was living helter-skelter on everyone else's property. What existed on legal paper and what existed on the open prairie were two completely different realities.

This could nevertheless be made to work—and was—as long as nobody became too bloody-minded about the legalities. But the mismatch didn't stop there. The Mennonites' village design wasn't based on mere aesthetics. It was based on a whole associated social system, a sort of semicommunal brotherhood, and this system too was completely out of step with the individualistic principles on which the law of Canada was based. The Mennonites' social system, in fact, was a mirror image of their church structure, which was run by Elders and church-associated or church-appointed officials, often rather autocratic, using a system of social incentives and discipline custom-designed to foster the Mennonite way of life. It worked fairly well—one suspects far better than Canada's legal system served the Mennonites in most instances—but Canada's legal system obviously had the upper hand.

The Manitoba Mennonites tried to sidestep their side of this paradox by making recourse to Canada's law courts a religious offence—and if Mennonites were inadvertently caught up in the net of Canadian law (for instance, arrested or charged by the RCMP—not that this happened very often, since the church's rules tended to be more strict than Canada's), they were instructed to promptly plead guilty regardless of actual guilt, pay their fine, and in this way quickly and quietly extricate themselves from an authority the Mennonites wanted little or nothing to do with. The law, on the other hand, couldn't really object since, for the record at least, it always got (or in this case was handed) its man.

It was a house of cards, and it wasn't long before the whole structure collapsed. The first fissures appeared in the West Reserve, where better soil made the intensive cultivation of wheat (and the resulting cash rewards) a great temptation. But since the Russian Mennonites' social structure had always been based on a principle of self-sufficiency and the greatest good for the greatest number, many Mennonites were uneasy about risking everything on a single cash crop. Self-sufficiency had always meant a mixed economy, with dairy and poultry products, vegetables and a variety of grain crops rather than just wheat. The debate became heated.

In any given village, it only took one rebellious Mennonite to bring everything down. One man insisting on his legal land rights obliged the RCMP to consider villagers living or cultivating anywhere on his 160 acres as squatters. Given the cohesive layout of the villages, that could easily affect most if not all of the villagers. And even when it didn't, in the uproar that followed, others often took the opportunity to "go individual" too. Village after village disbanded, each family moving or rebuilding its house on its own quarter section. By 1900,

David Peters and family, Gretna, Manitoba, 1890 (MHC)

Facing page: *Woman sitting in a garden* (CMBSC ARCHIVES)

only twenty-six years after their arrival in Manitoba, the Mennonites' close-habitat/open-field system, and most of their associated line villages, had been largely abandoned or dismantled.

Mennonite Social Institutions

A similar if less disastrous mismatch existed between the Mennonites and the provincial/municipal administrative structures. Since the Russian Mennonites had emigrated to Manitoba as whole colonies, their groups had arrived complete with mayors (Schulze), fire-chiefs (Brandschulze), and village assemblies (Schulzenbott) in place—all of whom had promptly carried on in these capacities in Manitoba. As they'd been accustomed to do, the colonies proceeded to build roads, schools and similar communal facilities with communal labour and taxes which they raised themselves, without reference to any provincial or municipal legislation. This worked well for a while, since at this early stage in Manitoba's development there were few provincial statutes to contravene anyway, and in any case, the province hadn't yet been divided into municipalities. When it was, the East Reserve was simply rechristened the Municipality of Hanover, and the existing Oberschulze (mayor of all village mayors), now officially rechristened a "reeve," carried on business as usual. So far so good.

Unfortunately, a similar solution for the West Reserve, in which the reigning Oberschulze simply became the reeve of the Municipality of Rhineland, ran into difficulties when the reeve fell out with his church Elder and was excommunicated. This meant, of course, that no other colony member was permitted to have anything whatsoever to do with him—not much of a basis on which to try to conduct municipal business. Furthermore, the church appointed a replacement Oberschulze, who, since he hadn't been elected in the provincially approved way, actually had no official authority. Eventually a marvellously baroque system was devised, in which an "elected" reeve (on the strength of a mere handful of votes, since few if any of the Mennonites voted) deferred to, or acted for, the area's de facto reeve (the Oberschulze), who, though he had no official provincial status, nevertheless instructed each village mayor on what was to be done.

This solution, however makeshift, worked acceptably enough for a while—but it too was doomed to eventual failure. As the power and authority of the more autocratic Elders waned, an increasing number of Mennonites risked church censure and began to vote in municipal and provincial elections. Increasingly, candidates who didn't have the sanction of the church won these elections, and in time, the church was no longer able to exert as much pressure on the direction of municipal affairs.

A final area of contention—one that was at this point really more of an administrative

nuisance, but that would in the years ahead prove to be the spark that lit the final fuse for many of Canada's more conservative Mennonites—was the matter of schools. Among the list of privileges the Russian Mennonites had been granted prior to their 1874 immigration was the right to set up and run their own schools—schools intended by them to ensure that their children's education included a healthy dose of religious instruction—all taught in the German language, which was the language of their church services. To make sure of this, the Mennonites hired their own teachers, who were examined and appointed by the church.

In time, the more progressive Mennonites began to feel that the quality of education being provided in their schools might be adequate for conservative Mennonites who weren't really interested in education, but wholly insufficient by Canadian standards. They wanted to avail themselves of the greater resources of English-language public schools. The conservative factions pointed out, also with some justification, that once the language barrier between the Mennonite and the "English" world had been breached, many further changes dangerous to their religious integrity would undoubtedly result.

If the two factions had simply been able to go their separate ways, the problem might have ended right there. But unfortunately, in certain parts of Manitoba both factions belonged to the same municipality. And this meant that, since the more conservative faction refused on religious principles to vote, the more progressive group was able to enact the School Act's provisions and cause a public school to be instituted at public expense—thereby forcing members of the conservative group to pay a municipal school tax *on top of* the private levy they were already paying for their own private school.

When the conservative Mennonites tried to challenge this state of affairs by using the government's 1874 promise of freedom of schooling for their children, everybody got a rude shock. It was discovered that the federal government's promise had been illegal. Schools, they were informed, fell under provincial jurisdiction.

For the next thirty years this problem—for the moment merely an internal one for the Mennonites, involving little more than money/taxes—simmered and stewed. Not until the First World War were the more explosive ingredients added that would result in major upheaval . . .

The Growth of Mennonite Towns

Mennonite church leaders had always favoured and promoted farming as the only occupation truly worthy of a Mennonite. But several factors combined to loosen such strictures at least a little. Towns along railroad lines—including lines across or alongside the Mennonite reserves—grew quickly, both as supply centres for surrounding farm communities and as

Mennonite children on the prairies, 1902
(CMBSC ARCHIVES)

shipping centres for local produce. The rapid growth of Mennonite families and farms provided a steady increase in business to these towns, and the Mennonite preference for doing business with other Mennonites eventually encouraged the gradual development of a merchant group there. Grist and flour mills had always been built and operated by Mennonites, but now they began expanding into such enterprises as machine shops, lumber yards, hardware stores, furniture factories and printing presses. Also, both the Russian colonies and the Prussian villages had always had a slightly larger percentage of tradesmen than most other Mennonite populations, and these also gravitated to the towns. By 1895 five large and rapidly expanding towns had been founded in the West Reserve (Rosenfeld, Gretna, Plum Coulee, Winkler and Altona), and by 1900 all of them had large Mennonite populations. In the East Reserve, Niverville, Gruenthal and Steinbach served the same functions.

Westward Expansion

As Mennonite families and their farms grew—both in Manitoba and southern Ontario—the need for new or additional agricultural land became ever greater. This was not only the result of the rapid growth of the many existing Canadian Mennonite communities but due also to a steady trickle of additional Mennonite immigrants to Ontario and Manitoba from Kansas, Minnesota, Nebraska, North Dakota, and even Prussia and Russia—especially after 1890. So when the Dominion government opened what was then the Northwest Territories (now Saskatchewan and Alberta) to immigrants on terms similar to those the Mennonites had received in 1874, thousands of Mennonites from all the aforementioned places—and Ontario and Manitoba too—availed themselves of these additional opportunities.

In contrast to the Mennonite immigration into Manitoba (and actually more like the 1786 Mennonite immigration into southwestern Ontario), these migrations were undertaken for the most part by smaller family or congregational groups. As new north-south rail lines were laid to connect with the existing east-west main lines, they pressed in from all sides—"Old" Mennonites from Ontario, Bergthaler Mennonites from Manitoba, Amish Mennonites from Iowa and Nebraska, Holdeman Mennonites from both Manitoba and Oregon, Mennonite Brethren in Christ settlers from Ontario, Old Colony Mennonites from Manitoba, and Rosenorter Mennonites from Prussia and Russia.

Saskatchewan, which was mostly settled by Dutch-German Mennonites, attracted the largest numbers, aided by the establishment of the Saskatchewan-Manitoba Land Company in 1902. A reserve was set aside for the Mennonites in the Carrot River Valley, east of Prince Albert. Old Colony Mennonites from Manitoba decided to take one more stab at open-field villages around the Hague and Warman area in 1895, and around Swift Current in 1904. In

The Abraham Willem farm near Patrofka, Saskatchewan, 1904 (CMBSC ARCHIVES)

Facing page: *Baden, Ontario, in 1920* (CGC ARCHIVES)

both cases they applied for and were granted Mennonite reserves in these areas as well. By 1905, Rosthern had already become one of the largest grain-shipping centres in Canada, and most of its grain was being grown by Prussian, Russian and American Dutch-German Mennonites.

In Alberta, which was settled mostly by Mennonites of Swiss-German background, attempts to have reserves earmarked for the Mennonites ran into resistance, and none were achieved, but plenty of settlements were founded anyway. Mennonites from Manitoba settled in Gleichen as early as 1891. In the same year, a group of Bergthalers from Manitoba moved to the Didsbury-Carstairs area, where they were joined by "Old" Mennonites and Mennonite Brethren in Christ from Ontario over the next four years. Their successes with sugar beets in this area were so impressive that they found themselves having to deal with a fair bit of competitive jealousy from non-Mennonite neighbours, a situation that took many years to smooth out. Further settlements were established in Linden, where Holdeman Mennonites from both Manitoba and Oregon joined forces in 1902, and in High River, with another group of "Old" Mennonites from Ontario. Some conservative Mennonites came all the way from Pennsylvania to start over in Duchess.

Basically, as soon as the railroads, the RCMP and the land agents opened up new country, the Mennonites were always close on their heels. In all, approximately forty Mennonite settlements were founded in Saskatchewan between 1890 and 1914. These were situated primarily in and around the two reserves already mentioned, and included Osler, Warman, Hague and Neuanlage, as well as Blumenhof, Schoenfeld, Shantzenfeld and Rosenort.

In Alberta, around sixteen settlements were established during that time, many between Red Deer and Calgary (including Didsbury, Carstairs, May City), as well as some northeast and southeast of these (High River, Gleichen, Tofield).

Canada-wide Statistics: 1913

By 1913 there were about 50,000 Mennonites living in Canada—about 13,000 in Ontario (which was experiencing a slight drop because of the westward migration of some of the Swiss-German Mennonites there), approximately 17,000 in Manitoba, 16,500 in Saskatchewan, 2,000 in Alberta and a few hundred in British Columbia. These numbers received a considerable boost during the next two years, as a flood of Mennonite conscientious objectors poured into Canada from the United States, fleeing harassment and intolerance during World War I.

Top: *Threshing in southern Manitoba, 1950s* (CARILLON NEWS ARCHIVES)

Bottom: *An early Mennonite home in Saskatchewan* (CANADIAN MENNONITE ARCHIVES)

Facing page: *Rosthern, Saskatchewan, in 1906* (MHC)

The Mennonites and World War I

The Mennonites and Military Service

The refusal to bear arms had always been an integral part of the Mennonites' pacifist principles, and an important element whenever they considered uprooting to another country. It had been promised them in both Russia and Pennsylvania, and formed part of their negotiations with the lieutenant-governor of Canada as early as 1774. A promise to that effect was finally extended by Canada in 1786, shortly after the American Revolution, though not formalized until the Militia Act of 1793. Various subsequent statutes and Orders in Council confirmed this exemption over the following 120 years.

Two Mennonite boys, 1918 (MHC)

The coming of the First World War threatened to steamroll over all these agreements. As pro-war propaganda swept through the land and emotions rose, the Mennonites' popularity began to slip. This was made worse by the fact that they not only spoke German but also had a German background. Public calls for their disenfranchisement and internment as enemy aliens grew louder. It wasn't long before many of their religious publications were censored and then suppressed altogether, under the existing War Measures Act. Mennonite evangelists trying to enter Canada from the U.S.A. to preach pacifism to Canadian Mennonite churches were turned back at the border or deported. In 1917 the Wartime Elections Act denied the vote to "enemy aliens" and conscientious objectors—anyone who voted automatically lost his military exemption. All during the war, Mennonite males of military age were harassed by the military bureaucracy, and Mennonite leaders were kept busy petitioning and negotiating to see that the law wasn't misused by overeager induction officials.

The Mennonites tried in vain to explain that they weren't being disloyal to Canada. Though they could not, according to their religious principles, engage in killing other human beings, they were quite willing to help those who had been victimized by war. They sent large donations—eventually totalling over a million dollars—to the Red Cross, as well as to Canada's Patriotic Fund, to be used to help war widows, victims and veterans. In one of the first instances of province-wide co-operation (after years of fracturing and dividing), Ontario Mennonite congregations joined forces to create the Non-Resistant Relief Organization, which gathered funds for this purpose. The Mennonites of Berlin, Ontario, changed their town's name to the more patriotic "Kitchener." A few Mennonites even enlisted, to the dismay of their Elders. But none of this did them much good in the public's eye.

The fact that the Mennonites had been specifically invited to Canada on negotiated and guaranteed conditions, both in 1786 and 1874, and had in both cases delivered precisely what the Canadian government had needed—successful homesteaders to settle and develop Canada's farmland—was conveniently forgotten. What Canadians now saw, from an increasingly jaundiced perspective, was a people who, having managed to negotiate all sorts of special privileges not available to other settlers, were nevertheless resisting assimilation and

Previous page: *Re-enactment of Mennonite emigrants leaving for Mexico in 1920, for the Mennonite film* And When They Shall Ask (MHC)

refusing to "defend" their country for religious reasons—while most other religious communities (such as the Catholics, Anglicans, Methodists) were very supportive of the war effort. The press called this the height of ingratitude. When some of the Mennonites unsuccessfully applied to the government to have further lands set aside for them in the Peace River district, to escape some of this pressure, the argument against them was that available land should first go to the war veterans. The Great War Veterans Association, and others, petitioned to have the Mennonites' military exemption rescinded.

More School Debacle

It was therefore no accident that Mennonite schools also came under renewed scrutiny and increasingly hostile assessment. Here were people of Germanic origin conducting schools in which English was an elective subject—schools that taught values and social guidelines not necessarily in keeping with the needs and aspirations of the British Empire. "What we need," announced Manitoba's Premier Rodmond Roblin, "is to get the youth filled with the traditions of the British flag, and then, when they are men . . . they will be able to defend it."

In Ontario, the Swiss-German Mennonites had reached a compromise with their provincial school boards by agreeing to make English the language of instruction and German an elective subject. But on the prairies, many of the conservative and more recent Dutch-German Mennonite settlers felt themselves threatened by what seemed to them a well-synchronized effort to anglicize, patriotize, militarize and secularize their children and ultimately themselves. Their more determined resistance resulted in a more determined governmental attack. So, when both Manitoba and Saskatchewan passed stiff new school acts shortly after the war which had the effect of abolishing the Mennonites' private bilingual schools completely and forcing their children to attend non-Mennonite public ones, almost one-third of the Mennonites in those two provinces responded as they had always responded to such confrontations. A delegation was sent to Latin America to search out a possible new home and a new future.

Exodus To Latin America

The press hysteria against the Mennonites increased steadily. Finally, in 1919, bowing to public pressure resulting mostly from media reports claiming that hundreds of thousands of additional conscientious objectors were preparing to immigrate to Canada from the United States, the Canadian government passed an Order in Council prohibiting any further immigration into Canada by groups such as the Mennonites, Hutterites and Doukhobors. (In due course this embargo was extended to blacks, Chinese and Japanese as well.) The province of Saskatchewan had already seized the lands of the Doukhobors for their refusal to comply with the existing school act in 1907; now Manitoba and Saskatchewan began fining and jailing Mennonites for noncompliance with the school act too. They even went so far as to hire or pay Mennonite informers to turn in their noncomplying coreligionists. Many Mennonite communities sustained deep and disastrous social fractures, some of which remain to this day.

By 1920 the decision to emigrate, arrived at after much doubt and agonizing, had become firm. During the following six years, some 6,000 Mennonites in Saskatchewan and Manitoba liquidated their farm holdings and left Canada for Mexico; over the next four, a further 1,800 left for Paraguay. Even after they had announced their intentions, and were only waiting until the sale of their farms and cattle could be completed, the school boards continued to fine and jail them.

The exodus to Latin America in the 1920s reduced the number of Mennonites in Canada back to their 1913 level—about 50,000 church members.

Meanwhile, Over in Russia . . .

While the Mennonites in Canada (and in the U.S.A. and Europe) were having a decidedly unpleasant time of it under increasing public (but still legally appealable) pressure between 1914 and 1918, their problems hardly compared with those of the Mennonites in Russia. The Russian Revolution that began in 1917 unleashed a rampage of havoc and slaughter throughout their once-prosperous colonies, as the Red and the White armies repeatedly crossed and crisscrossed the area, and Anarchist bands pillaged and destroyed what little was left. So devastating and vicious were these attacks that some Mennonites abandoned their pacifism and formed irregular self-protective brigades. It didn't make much difference. Tens of thousands were massacred; further thousands starved to death.

It wasn't until 1921 that the situation stabilized enough to allow Canadian, American and Dutch Mennonite aid to be delivered. This was accomplished by co-ordinating the work of many different Mennonite relief organizations under a single umbrella known as the Mennonite Central Committee, another early and highly successful practical effort to overcome the theological fracturing so endemic to the many different Mennonite congregational families. The MCC sent over millions of dollars' worth of food and financial aid, as well as seed grain and tractors, once the most immediate famine problems had been eased.

But the easing of the most immediate physical suffering didn't result in a return to normalcy. Normalcy—a return to the prosperity the Mennonite colonies had enjoyed in Russia

Boarding the emigration train to Paraguay, 1927 (MHC)

Facing page: *Emigration to Paraguay, on board ship, 1926* (MENNONITISCHE POST ARCHIVES)

for almost 150 years—was never to be had again. No sooner had the Russian Revolution resolved itself than land reform programmes began to strip the remaining Mennonites of their farms. The colonies were disintegrating. The pressure to emigrate became desperate once more. Delegations showed up on North America's doorstep, urgently seeking entrance.

As far as Canada was concerned, the situation was rather complicated. On the one hand, over 7,000 Mennonites had just vacated, or were in the process of vacating, their excellent farms all over Saskatchewan and Manitoba. As well, much of Alberta and British Columbia was still only sparsely populated, and the railway companies were anxious to find buyers for their lands in those provinces. On the other hand, there was the Order in Council of 1919. That, and public sentiment, were major obstacles to all petitioners.

Obviously, the federal government had to be convinced to change its mind. The railways lobbied vigorously. The Mennonites sent delegation after delegation to Ottawa. They stressed the differences between the Mennonites who had raised so much public anger in the prairies (known hereafter as the "Ausswanderer" or "emigrant" group) and those who now wanted entrance. The Russian Mennonites of the 1920s (or "Russlaender" as they were called, to differentiate them from the Mennonites of Russian origin who had immigrated to Canada in 1874, hereafter called "Kanadier") were far more progressive than the Ausswanderer who were leaving. The Russlaender were generally well educated, already bilingual and unafraid of the challenges of trilingualism. They had already demonstrated their resourcefulness once and would do so again. Furthermore, they would be taken care of by the remaining 50,000 Canadian Mennonites, in both Ontario and western Canada.

In the end, it was mostly the Swiss-German Mennonites of Ontario who carried the day. Their public image was at the time more "presentable," and they just happened to be among Liberal Opposition Leader Mackenzie King's constitutents (King had lived among the Mennonites, and liked them). When King became prime minister in 1923, he quietly passed an Order in Council to lift the ban. This enabled the Canadian Mennonite Board of Colonization, which had already been formed in anticipation of this possibility, to go into action.

Dramatic Rescue Mission

It proved the biggest undertaking of its kind in Mennonite history. The Board of Colonization teamed up with the Canadian Pacific Railway, signing transportation contracts that eventually totalled over two million dollars to rescue almost 23,000 Mennonites over a seven-year period between 1923 and 1930. It was a trying time for everyone. Attempting to synchronize such international efforts between increasingly hostile countries through complicated bureaucracies proved enormously difficult; many times, misunderstandings, delays or

Immigrants boarding trains in Europe, on their way to Canada (MHC)

Facing page: *Immigrants being given a medical check before entering Canada, 1923* (MHC)

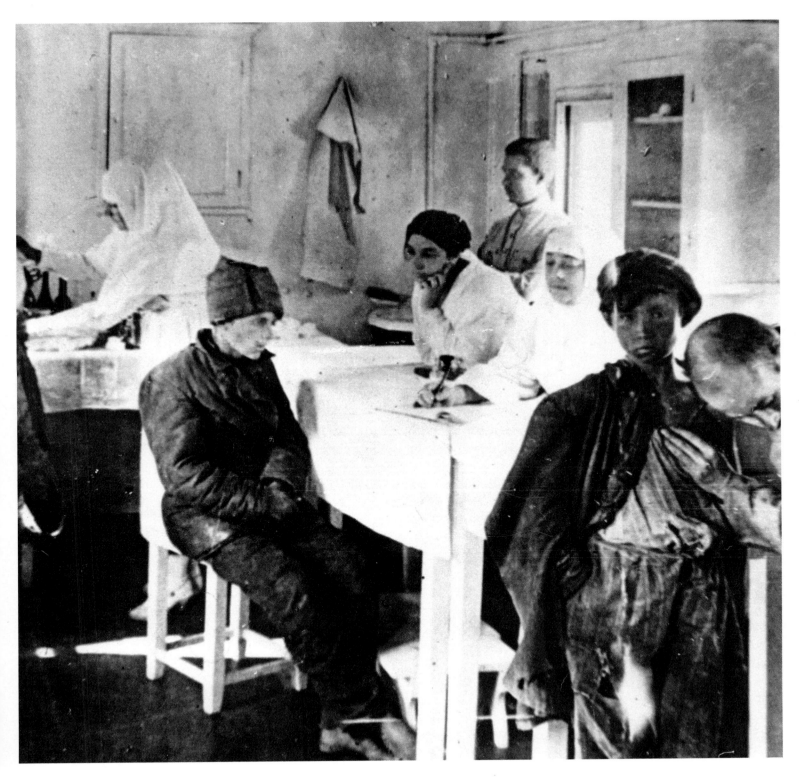

unexplained cancellations made the entire enterprise seem doomed. Outbreaks of cholera and trachoma delayed and almost scuppered the passage of most of the earliest groups. Russian petulance made passports increasingly difficult to get. The costs of accommodating and curing those Mennonites unable to pass the Canadian medical examinations became enormous.

Fortunately the German government began contributing to the rescue mission from its third year on, permitting Mennonites temporary sanctuary in Germany while on their way to Canada and paying for their medical and physical care during that time. (When Canada's doors eventually closed again in 1931, the Germans even financed a modest continuation of the rescue mission to Brazil and Paraguay.)

The huge CPR transportation debt, and many ancillary settlement costs besides, were underwritten by contributions from Mennonites all over Canada; and though there was also a lot of opposition to such a potentially ruinous financial committment, charity eventually overcame fiscal caution. The debt itself was expected to be repaid over time by the new immigrants themselves, which in large measure it was, though the Depression and other stumbling blocks made several renegotiations and extensions necessary.

One of the stipulations laid down by the Canadian government in 1923 had been that the new immigrants settle on farmland, because jobs in Canadian cities were already becoming scarce. This wasn't considered much of a limitation, since most Mennonites were still farmers. However, there were few good plots of land left within reasonable reach of railroad spur lines. Furthermore, though most Russlaender immigrants had been landowners or farmers of means in Russia, few had been able to rescue or liquidate their assets and were quite poor. Various innovative means therefore had to be found to make it possible for them to acquire farms.

To make this happen, the CPR's Canadian Colonization Association teamed up with the Mennonite Land Settlement Board to bring buyers and sellers of land together. Where farms vacated by the Ausswanderer became available, the board assisted in their purchase by Russlaender. The board's agents also searched western Canada for likely looking plots of land still available through government land grants.

There was also a third and more unusual high-risk option that was tried with variable success over the following several decades. A considerable number of huge, often fully equipped farms—between 4,000 to 10,000 acres—were coming onto the market as farm prices dropped in the 1920s. Though much too large for a single family, about 65 such farms were bought by various groups of Russlaender, their plan being to work them communally until sufficient prosperity allowed them to split them up into many smaller farms. The only problem with this option was that the debt loads were so huge, a single crop failure could spell bankruptcy—a fate that befell over a quarter of such undertakings.

Top and bottom: *Russian Mennonites arriving in Ontario, 1924* (CGC ARCHIVES)

Facing page: *Arrival of the first group of Russian Mennonites in Rosthern, Saskatchewan, 1923* (CMBSC ARCHIVES)

Many Russlaender had to work for wages for a few years before being able to sign mortgages for farms. They found jobs as harvesters (at $5 per day), railroad labourers ($3 per day plus board), or workers in sawmills or mining camps ($35 per month plus room and board). Some took factory or construction jobs in the cities at 15 to 25 cents per hour and eventually just stayed there. This led to some friction, especially in Ontario, where about 1,500 Russlaender had settled in and around Waterloo, New Hamburg and Hespeler, and where competition for wage jobs was stiff. Many of these Russlaender eventually worked on or bought small fruit or tobacco farms in places like the Vineland-Beamsville area. In Manitoba, in a similar semi-urban situation, the district of North Kildonan (now part of Winnipeg) was eventually settled by hundreds of Russlaender who raised chickens and vegetables for Winnipeg residents on small one- to ten-acre plots.

But most Russlaender Mennonites wanted and settled on farms. When homestead land was no longer available, they took a chance on inexpensive CPR land in such areas as the northern Saskatchewan bushlands (North Battleford and environs), or dryland sugar-beet farms in southern Alberta (Coaldale). The discovery of excellent wheat-growing land in northern Alberta's isolated Peace River district attracted not only the Russlaender but Kanadier and Swiss-German and even American Mennonites, who wanted a greater separation from the secular world than was becoming possible in the more populated parts of Manitoba, Ontario, Oregon and Kansas.

For some years the most utopian dreams were reserved for the settlement of Reesor in northern Ontario. Here, land was available for 50 cents an acre, and the government was sufficiently eager to have it settled that permission was even given to create the traditional Russian-style closed-system villages. At its height Reesor boasted 226 persons on fifty-five homesteads, but swampy land and transportation difficulties eventually caused it to die out.

The Mennonites had better luck in southern British Columbia's Fraser Valley, where a Russian-style Mennonite village was established by the Russlaender in 1928 and named Yarrow. Here, on land reclaimed from a drained lake (eerily reminiscent of the Mennonites' early heritage in the Vistula delta in Prussia), the Mennonites tried sugar beets, beans, asparagus and peas without success, but finally hit the mark with raspberries and strawberries. Prosperity quickly followed, and additional arrivals spread into nearby Greendale, Chilliwack, Abbotsford and Clearbrook. The first Mennonite church was established in Vancouver in 1929.

By the early 1930s, the 20,000 new Russlaender Mennonites had thus settled into more than 270 different districts in Canada: 17 in Ontario, 89 in Manitoba, 108 in Saskatchewan, 43 in Alberta and 15 in British Columbia.

The Shantz button factory in Ontario, circa 1900 (MHC)

Facing page: *Threshing in Saskatchewan, 1920s* (CMBSC ARCHIVES)

A pioneer log cabin near Reesor in northern Ontario (MHC)

Facing page: *Pioneering near Reesor in northern Ontario* (MHC)

Clearing the land, Yarrow, B.C. (AGATHA KLASSEN)

Left: *Early days in Yarrow: picking hops in nearby Chilliwack, B.C.* (AGATHA KLASSEN)

Facing page: *The Epp children on Eckert Street, in Yarrow, B.C.* (AGATHA KLASSEN)

Between the Wars

The Impact of the Russlaender

The coming of the Russlaender Mennonites changed the face of Mennonitism in Canada once again—especially in western Canada. For one thing, their large numbers and tendency to group together virtually doubled the number of Mennonite congregations in Canada overnight. Between 1923 andd 1930, 176 new congregations were created by the Russlaender Mennonites alone.

For another, though they shared a common religious heritage, the many different groups of Mennonites often found more to disagree than to agree about. This was as true for the new Russlaender immigrants as it had been for the various Mennonite immigrations before them. From the Kanadier perspective, the Russlaender seemed a trifle too brash—too convinced of the merits of higher education, too inclined to take over positions of leadership, too ready to urbanize, too willing to co-operate with government, too inclined to take the Kanadier for granted. From the Russlaender perspective, the Kanadier tended to be to be too uninvolved with public and cultural life, too uncultured, too uneducated and unnecessarily narrow-minded.

As for the relationship between the Russlaender and the Ontario Mennonites (who hosted some 1,500 Russlaender for periods up to six months), the disparities were even greater, though this actually had the effect, in some instances, of making co-operation easier. Language constituted the most immediate barrier. Though Pennsylvania Deutsch and Low German share common roots, their differences nevertheless outweigh the similarities. Also, the fact that some Ontario Mennonites used their domestic dialect even for church services had an estranging effect on the Russlaender, for whom High German was the only acceptable language inside a church. Secondly, the Ontario Mennonites tended to live and worship plainly and simply, and for them the Russlaender's more liberal, educated and cosmopolitan outlook (not to mention dress, styles of worship and lifestyle) sometimes seemed to border on the heretical. And hadn't the Russlaender, after all, even agreed to wartime service in the Russian Army's medical corps, and taken up weapons to form self-defence brigades against the Anarchist raiders?

It was therefore no surprise that while relations remained cordial, the Russlaender soon formed their own churches in Ontario or headed west to the prairies where the greater number of their own group had settled.

Interestingly, the Mennonites among whom the Russlaender tended most predictably to find kindred spirits were the Prussian and American Mennonite immigrants of 1890–1920, many of whom had settled in Saskatchewan and Alberta. It was often with these, who shared their enthusiasm for education and organization, that they made common cause in soon establishing, or causing to be established, a large number of bible schools and institutions—133

A funeral procession in Manitoba, 1930s (MHC)

Previous page: *Transporting children to summer bible school, Baden, Ontario, 1935* (CGC ARCHIVES)

A Mennonite wedding in southern Saskatchewan, circa 1920 (CMBSC ARCHIVES)

Right: *A funeral in Eyebrow, Saskatchewan, 1930* (CMBSC ARCHIVES)

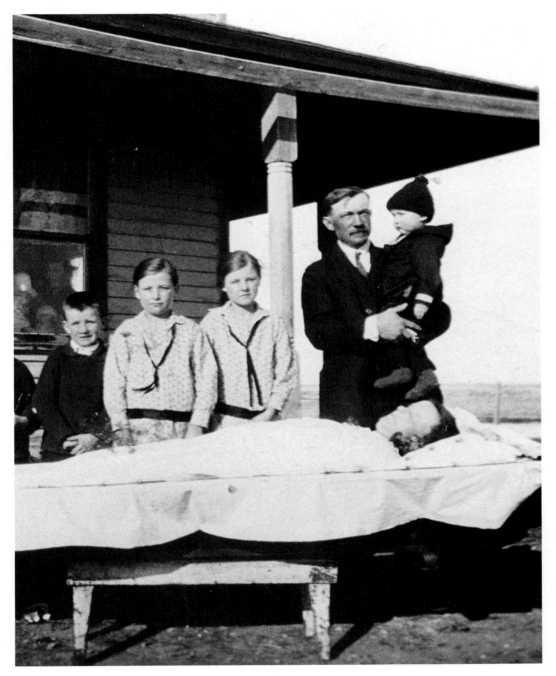

of them—in such cities and towns as Kitchener and Virgil in Ontario; Winnipeg, Winkler and Gretna in Manitoba; Hepburn in Saskatchewan, Coaldale in Alberta and Yarrow in British Columbia.

Fortunately for everyone, the three main denominational orientations with which the Russlaender arrived already existed in similar form in Canada, or there might have been even greater denominational fracturing than there was already. These were the Mennonite Conference, the Mennonite Brethren and the Mennonite Alliance. (The Alliance, which was eventually absorbed into the Mennonite Brethren group, was essentially a more flexible and ecumenical form of the latter.) The differences between the Conference and the Brethren churches, however, was seen as sufficiently important that most new Russlaender settlements across Canada ended up having both.

Another development directly attributable to the Russlaender immigration was the establishment, by the General Conference of the Mennonite Church of North America, of a system of paid "Reiseprediger" (itinerant preachers) to serve the many small and far-flung congregations (primarily Russlaender) throughout central and western Canada. These preachers were usually Russlaender Elders who, having lost everything in the Russian colonies, were now insolvent and without a ministry. They were generally paid the meagre monthly allowance of $50, and their work load was enormous. One such minister, F. F. Enns, recorded the following activities over a fourteen-month stretch:

"Preached 192 times at 69 places; Communion to 1267 souls at 16 places; Baptism for 32 souls at 4 places; Ordained 3 preachers and 1 deacon; Attended at 3 elections—5 ministers & 1 bishop; Worked away from home 206 days; Visited 424 families at 69 places; Travelled 1596 miles by wagon and sleigh; Travelled 5832 miles by train; Travelled 27 miles on foot; Four marriages; Gave medicine to 273 persons."

Russlaender Church Services and Administration

For the Russlaender, as for all other Mennonites at this time, the church remained the centre of their spiritual and social life—particularly since Mennonites still shunned, to one degree or another, worldly amusements and secular social organizations. The church was thus the source of their identity, their social status, their community and their fellowship. This had been true since the sixteenth century and remained true despite many changes in methods of worship and church administration.

Generally speaking, worship services included one or several sermons preached in High German (eventually English) every Sunday, as well as on holidays and special festival days such as Good Friday, Easter, Epiphany, Ascension Day and so on. Prayer meetings and bible

Top: *The Burns Ranch G.C. Mennonite Church, near Didsbury, Alberta, 1934* (KATHY PETERS)

Bottom: *Sunday afternoon, southern Manitoba, 1938* (PATRICK FRIESEN)

Facing page: *Preparing the fields for sugar beets, southern Alberta, 1939* (PETER TOEWS)

study sessions were offered weekly (in the evenings), and once a year, a two- to three-day bible conference was conducted by a visiting minister. Visiting evangelists were also invited, usually once a year, to conduct two- to five-day revival meetings.

Most congregations had a chorister who selected the hymns and started the singing on the right note or pitch (eventually with the support of a pianist or even an organist) from his seat in the front pew or up front with the ministers. Singing tended to be in four-part harmony. In time, church choirs, who sat as a group either behind the ministers at the front (facing the congregation) or in a balcony at the back of the church, became common.

The high point in the congregation's life was the celebration of baptism, which usually occurred in the candidate's late teens and which also constituted entry into the congregation as a fully fledged member. Communion, celebrated only several times a year, was intended not only to commemorate Christ's death but also to encourage the resolution of internal strife or discord. A special sermon exhorting members towards that end was usually preached a Sunday in advance, and everyone was expected to have resolved their differences by the following Sunday. Nonparticipation thus implied the inability or refusal to "straighten out" one's life, and was viewed with a great deal of seriousness and concern.

Most Russlaender congregations were administered by the "Bruderschaft" (Brotherhood), an assembly of all the male members of the church—though female members were gradually being included as well. The Brotherhood elected both the congregation's spiritual leaders (Elder, ministers, deacons) as well as a church council of three to five members, who looked after the congregation's business affairs.

In view of the many theological perspectives within the various Mennonite churches, it became increasingly common to set down a congregation's creed in a formal constitution. This ensured a clear understanding of the biblical doctrines upon which such a creed was based, as well as the congregation's particular conditions for membership, the duties involved, and its disciplinary and electoral procedures. While such constitutions were less common among the Kanadier congregations, most Russlaender congregations established them right from the start.

The Great Depression

No one needs to be told how hard the Dirty Thirties were on Canada's prairie farmers. The images of sky-high funnels of dust and grasshoppers, caterpillar infestations, unrelenting heat and so little rain that even during winter's subzero temperatures, there wasn't enough moisture in the soil to freeze the dust—these have been burned into Canada's collective memory through many books and films. Wheat prices plummeted from a 1929 high of $1.13

A Mennonite family at mealtime, Alberta (MHC)

Facing page: *A Mennonite Brethren baptismal service near Hepburn, Saskatchewan, 1952* (PETER TOEWS)

per bushel to a 1932 low of 19 cents. Cattle and hog prices fell through the bottom in much the same way. There was no unemployment insurance to offset a national unemployment rate as high as 23 per cent. Thousands of farmers lost their farms.

The prairie Mennonites were hit broadside by the Depression. In the 1930s there were more than 30,000 Mennonites living in Saskatchewan alone, at least half of whom had settled in areas that eventually became the dust bowl. In Manitoba's West Reserve, over 6,000 farmers were in serious danger of losing title to their lands by 1936. The Russlaender, who had only barely settled into their jobs or farms, were hit particularly hard.

The Loss of the "Banks with a Heart"

The disaster didn't extend merely to farms and produce prices. The effects of the Depression shook up many financial institutions, organizations and schemes, and when the shaking stopped, many had collapsed. Some of the first to disintegrate were the venerable Waisenamts, the informal Orphans' Funds used by many Mennonite congregations as a "bank with a heart." These funds, which had been created primarily to protect the estate interests of Mennonite orphans and widows, had also become popular places for Mennonites to invest their savings. Such savings were then loaned to other, more needy Mennonites, at very low interest rates. While the interest paid to the depositors was consequently also very modest, the knowledge that their money was being used to help less fortunate Mennonites normally kept the Waisenamts easily solvent. And since paying one's debts was high on the list of a Mennonite's social and religious duties, bad debts under ordinary circumstances happened rarely enough to make the whole operation quite manageable.

But no one had calculated disasters such as a major depression into the formula. And when the stock market crashed and produce prices plummeted, people needed money and tried to withdraw their savings in amounts the Waisenamts couldn't cover. Worse, outstanding loans couldn't be collected for precisely the same reason. Like banks without the necessary reserves, many of the Waisenamts collapsed like houses of cards, taking trust and traditions with them.

Bad and worse followed. The Intercontinental Land Company, which had been formed by non-Mennonite financiers to buy up large sections of Ausswanderer lands for resale to the incoming Russlaender, was foreclosed upon and collapsed, taking with it the invested savings of almost a thousand Ontario and U.S.A. Mennonites, who had been convinced to assist in the immigration plans for the Russlaender in this way.

Worse almost than such financial losses, one creditor was later to say, was the change they caused in the way people conducted business with each other after the Depression. Until then, Mennonites had rarely bothered with contracts and legal documents, especially with

The Abraham C. Fehr family, heading back to Hague, Saskatchewan, after an unsuccessful attempt to start again in the Peace River area, 1934 (Glenbow Archives, Calgary, Alberta)

Facing page: *After a locust attack* (CARILLON NEWS ARCHIVES)

each other. A man's word was his bond, and an Elder's judgement resolved any differences. Such cordial, casual forms of commerce took a fatal beating during the thirties. And with it, yet another beneficial influence of the church was lost.

Self-Help and Mutual Aid—Church Version

The collapse of the Waisenamts had the effect of alerting the Mennonites to possible problems with some of their other mutual-aid institutions too. Their various forms of self-financed, nonprofit and therefore very economical fire insurance plans came under close scrutiny, and many of them were eventually reorganized and/or incorporated under conventional charters. A church-financed automobile accident insurance plan was even considered, though dropped because of excessive costs. What did come into being in those days before government medical insurance was a variety of medical benefit plans, also nonprofit, very affordable and operated entirely by Mennonites for Mennonites. In Ontario the Mennonite Mutual Benefit Association provided its members with "a systematic method of sharing, in a Christian way, the financial burdens of sickness, disability and death." In western Canada, Mennonite hospital societies took this approach a considerable step farther, with the direct hiring of Mennonite doctors and the establishment of Mennonite hospitals (and eventually senior citizens' homes as well). In such a system, $18 per year could provide an entire family with complete medical care. (As usual, most of these societies too were organized along denominational lines.)

The Depression encouraged the formation or reactivation of a considerable number of Mennonite church-sponsored aid organizations, such as the Non-Resistant Relief Organization (Ontario, 1937), the Mennonite Welfare Board (Ontario, 1939), the Mennonite Central Relief Committee (Manitoba, 1940), and the Canadian Mennonite Relief Committee (Manitoba, 1940). Many of these, and other Mennonite organizations like them, would eventually amalgamate their parallel and overlapping functions under the umbrella of the Mennonite Central Committee–Canada.

Self-Help and Mutual Aid—Secular Version

One of the almost instinctive solutions many Mennonites initiated or availed themselves of during the thirties and forties, both to offset the Depression and to get back onto their feet afterward, was the co-operative.

Co-operatives had already existed in a small way before the Depression, but with the

The Zoar Senior Citizens' Home, Yarrow, B.C., 1946 (AGATHA KLASSEN)

Facing page: *"At Mother's grave," Elbow, Saskatchewan, 1940s* (CMBSC ARCHIVES)

steady diminishing of church controls and the collapse of such church self-help institutions as the Waisenamt, secular equivalents like co-operatives became increasingly appealing. From Virgil, Ontario, where a fruit-growers' co-op helped maintain reasonable prices and avoid excessive spoilage, to a Yarrow, B.C. fruit-growers' co-op that expanded to include a feed/grain buying business and a berry preserving/packing plant, Mennonite co-operatives sprang up everywhere to assist in the processing and marketing of eggs, cheese, fruit, cream, vegetables, grains, hogs and cattle. They were also used to cut costs in the purchase of machine parts, clothing and farm hardware. In Altona, Manitoba, a group of sixty-seven farmers reduced their gasoline and oil costs by buying a filling station, enabling them to purchase their fuel supplies in bulk. That co-op too grew to include many ancillary ventures; many co-operatives became sufficiently successful to become credit unions.

In these and similar ways, the Mennonites tackled their share in these disasters largely on their own. Few ended up on the welfare rolls. Mennonites less affected, such as those living in Ontario or British Columbia, quickly pitched in with entire railcar-loads of produce and clothing—not only for their fellow Mennonites but non-Mennonites as well. In Mennonite villages or towns, people pulled together as never before. Church members were urged to see their ministers or deacons before considering government relief, and usually a solution was found "in-house." The Mennonites, after all, had had plenty of practice throughout their history in dealing with such situations.

As farmers, they reverted wherever possible to what they had until comparatively recently always pursued anyway—mixed farming. Instead of a single cash crop, they diversified into dairy and chicken/egg production, fruit and vegetable gardens, and the raising of hogs and slaughter-cattle. Those who couldn't maintain their farms even under those conditions—in southern Saskatchewan for example—moved farther north, or to British Columbia (the Fraser Valley) or Ontario (the Niagara Peninsula). The movement to British Columbia, in fact, began a trend that didn't stop even after the Depression years were over.

The thirties saw one last sizable attempt to establish a large-scale Mennonite settlement far from the populated world and its dust bowls. Tentatively optimistic reports from a small number of Mennonite settlers in the vast and fertile Peace River district of northern Alberta had been heard with interest in a number of Mennonite communities, and in 1934 a 300-family remnant of the Saskatchewan Rheinlaender group (about a thousand of whom had emigrated to Mexico in 1924) decided to give it a try near the town of Fort Vermilion. They were joined in due course by a number of returnees from Mexico, where relations between the government and the Mennonites had deteriorated for all the usual reasons, and where Mennonite villages were being attacked by bandit groups emboldened by the Mennonites' pacifism. The hoped-for massing of Mennonites in the Peace never came about, though a sprinkling of permanent settlements did become established. By 1941 the Mennonite presence in the district had grown to some 450 families.

The Yarrow berry co-operative, Yarrow, B.C. (AGATHA KLASSEN)

An early co-operative cheese factory, Coaldale, Alberta, 1937 (AGNES HUBERT)

Right: *A co-op in difficulties, Rosenort, Manitoba, 1940* (CARILLON NEWS ARCHIVES)

The Mennonites and World War II

Renewed Soul-Searching

With the end of the Depression and the rise in international hostilities once more, the Mennonites seemed headed straight into the same storm they had experienced during World War I—and in many ways this was so. True, this time they were in good company; WWI had changed many people's minds on this subject, and there were now large and very aggressive antiwar groups trying to avoid a repeat. Though the Mennonites refused to join such groups, they became very busy themselves, holding antiwar conferences, sending briefs and petitions to both Canadian government and foreign officials, and searching their own souls on the subject.

The soul-searching was necessary because the Mennonites' stand on nonresistance/ pacifism/nonviolence couldn't necessarily be taken for granted any more. The steady process of assimilation over the previous two decades had resulted in many changes within the Mennonite world, and in a few of its conferences (such as Ontario's Mennonite Brethren in Christ), there was even talk of eliminating the word "Mennonite"—which some congregations were finding a problem in their missionary efforts among non-Mennonite Canadians— from their church title altogether. Such congregations didn't seem to want to be particularly "separate" from the world any more.

As it turned out, most Mennonites did retain their pacifist traditions. What changed in some conferences was the view on "noncombatant alternative service," which all Mennonites who had come to Canada later than the Kanadier immigration of 1874 were obliged to perform. The Mennonites deliberated long and hard about whether alternative service was just another way of contributing to war. The topic became sufficiently hot that many fractures again threatened—and the Mennonite Central Relief Committee did eventually split over the issue.

In the end, they had to agree to disagree. Some churches, particularly the Russlaender congregations who had already become accustomed to such alternative service in Russia, had no great objection to this requirement. Early Kanadier and many Swiss-German Mennonites in Ontario felt otherwise.

When the Second World War began, roughly 7,500 Mennonites received conscientious objector status and served time in C-O logging camps, or were individually assigned to work in mines, on farms, in hospitals or mental institutions. Some were lucky enough to be assigned to farming duties on their own or relatives' farms. An inter-Mennonite Peace Committee was formed to minister to all Mennonite C-Os. As had happened in the previous war, the Mennonites also contributed large amounts of food, clothing and money towards the relief of war victims. This time around, the accusations of shirking civic responsibility and profiteering

Top: *A Conscientious Objectors' camp, Jasper, Alberta, 1942* (MHC)

Bottom: *A military service exemption certificate* (MHC)

Facing page: *Inside a Conscientious Objectors' camp during World War II* (CMBSC)

Previous page: *Mennonite children lining up for a meal in the embarkation hall at Bremen, Germany, circa 1948* (CMBSC ARCHIVES)

from the war were more muted, and people seemed to understand the Mennonites' position and history a little better.

Yet to everyone's surprise, and to the Mennonites' consternation, about 4,500 Mennonite men voluntarily enlisted in the armed forces—another painful indication to Mennonite leaders of how far the secularization of their flock had progressed.

Exodus Once More

Not only Mennonite leaders were appalled—the entire congregations of a number of the more conservative Kanadier churches felt they had seen this writing on the wall for some time. The steady incursions of "modernism" into the Mennonite fold, their inability to restrain Mennonite youth from the temptations of radios, automobiles, telephones and the English language, and now this—devastating proof that their faith was in more danger than ever before. Between 1946 and 1948 some 2,000 of them sold their farms and possessions and headed south to join their coreligionists in Paraguay.

And as irony would have it, in virtual parallel to the similar situation following World War I, Canada's immigration doors opened once again, virtually without warning, allowing in about 8,000 new Mennonite refugees from Europe. They came primarily from the badly disintegrated colonies in Russia, but also from Prussia (now Poland), where their villages had been completely overrun by the Russians in 1943. (In fact, WWII put an end to a Mennonite presence in Prussia, and left only a small scattering of Mennonite villages in Russia intact.) These latest refugees settled mainly in Alberta and in British Columbia, bringing Canada's 1951 Mennonite count to 126,000 (not counting unbaptized children).

Arnold Regier and Menno Geddert leave Bremen, Germany, bound for Canada, 1951 (H. CORNELSEN)

Facing page: *Mennonite immigrants detrain in Bremen, Germany, en route to Canada, 1948* (CMBSC ARCHIVES)

Top: *Back to school: Prussian Mennonite immigrants tackle the English language, Agassiz, B.C., 1952* (GERTRAUT HOERR)

Bottom: *The Canadian Pacific ship, the Beaverbrae, brought many Mennonites to Canada between 1948 and 1952* (CMBSC ARCHIVES)

Right: *Heinrich and Johanna Bartel, bound from Germany to Canada on the Beaverbrae, 1952* (GERTRAUT HOERR)

Facing page: *Embarking at Bremen, Germany, en route to Canada, circa 1948* (CMBSC ARCHIVES)

A final sermon before entraining for Paraguay, 1948 (MENNONITISCHE POST ARCHIVES)

Facing page: *Mennonites leaving for Paraguay, 1948* (MENNONITISCHE POST ARCHIVES)

The Erosion of Mennonite "Separateness"

In many ways, the effects of World War II were just as overwhelming for the Mennonites as their Old Order leaders had warned they would be. Change, which had been gathering speed among them, now virtually catapulted them into the technological age. Farming, once an old-fashioned family-size occupation, rapidly evolved into a highly mechanized, mega-dollar enterprise. Farmers who resisted the trend were swamped by the passing tidal wave. Those who didn't, found themselves obliged to operate their farms like modern businesses. The financial stakes kept rising. The Mennonites' traditional, almost sacred, sense of tilling the soil began to take a severe beating.

At the same time, the prosperity and sharply increased economic activity of the 1950s and '60s drew more and more Mennonites from the farms and into the cities. Such a move had already been pioneered by some of the 1920s Russlaender and by the daughters of Mennonite farmers who had worked in the cities as domestics. Now, augmented by the most recent Mennonite refugees from Europe, many of whom didn't even attempt to farm, and by the returned Mennonite soldiers and conscientious objectors, whose horizons had been sharply widened by their experiences in the "English" secular world, the urban Mennonite count rose sharply—so sharply, in fact, that already by 1960 the balance had tipped, and the majority of Mennonites were no longer farmers.

The Effects of Higher Education

By now, progressive Russlaender and Prussian Mennonites constituted more than half the Mennonite population of Canada, and their enterprising, take-charge approach was exercising a considerable influence on Mennonite affairs. Their interest in education, for example, had added the decisive push in the widespread creation of academically oriented Mennonite high schools and colleges (as opposed to bible schools) in the 1940s. With greater options open to them, the graduates of these schools also tended to gravitate to the cities and to enter many professions formerly "disencouraged" by the Mennonites. Even so, most of these professions fell within the "service" or "practical" sector—a sector philosophically closest to Mennonite traditions: nursing, medical school, dentistry, teaching, social work. But the result here too was an outward movement into the larger secular world. In rapid stages, Mennonite "separateness" was becoming eroded.

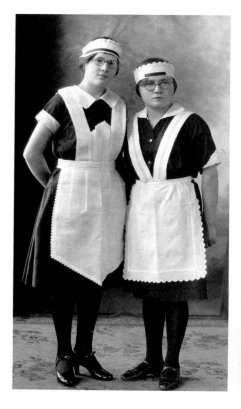

Mennonite domestics working in Winnipeg, 1940s (CMBSC ARCHIVES)

Facing page: *Mennonite farmers in southern Alberta combining forces to help out a sick fellow farmer, 1950s* (CARILLON NEWS ARCHIVES)

Previous page: *Different worlds: Old Order Mennonites harvest in the jet age* (KITCHENER-WATERLOO RECORD/ CGC ARCHIVES)

A Mennonite literary society drama production in Steinbach, Manitoba, 1957 (CARILLON NEWS ARCHIVES)

Right: *At a Brunk revival meeting, Winnipeg, Manitoba, 1957* (CMBSC ARCHIVES)

Facing page: *A Mennonite wedding in southern Saskatchewan, early 1950s* (CMBSC ARCHIVES)

The Arts and Culture

The preoccupation with higher education gave rise to an extraordinary phenomenon in the thirties and forties: the Mennonite literary societies. For a people who had throughout their history largely ignored or actively discouraged budding writers in their ranks—story-writing, for instance, was commonly associated with the telling of lies ("inventing")—this constituted a remarkable development. Some societies were church-sponsored, some weren't. They featured public speakers, debating sessions, book discussions, public speaking practice, bible study, social games, and even the performance of religious or domestic plays. Church leaders in general were never quite comfortable with these compromises between the constraints of church-supervised programmes and the temptations of secular cultural events in the "English" world, and their existence sometimes led to a lot of friction. A little less controversy (but only a little) surrounded the creation of church and secular choirs and music festivals, for which the Mennonites have since become justly renowned.

Involvement in Business

Not only education and the arts but the postwar business world too encouraged assimilative tendencies among the Mennonites. Since the turn of the century, the Mennonites had been establishing more and more agrarian-oriented small businesses—if only to serve their own communities where such services were lacking. Farm implement dealerships, filling stations, flour mills, cheese factories, small construction concerns, trucking, printing, real estate—businesses in which their traditional family and community values could be readily applied. The postwar demand for goods and services offered an irresistible welter of opportunities to expand and diversify these businesses, and the Mennonites didn't hesitate for long. Besides, a ready supply of cheap labour among the recent Mennonite refugees and those Mennonites who didn't want to farm any more made the manufacture of everything from construction supplies to home furnishings a profitable proposition.

Such changes, of course, were bound to affect the church as well. The now widespread Sunday schools and bible schools, which had become the testing grounds for new church leaders and administrators—including in particular Mennonite women, who were reaching beyond their sewing circles and volunteer groups to become missionaries and deaconesses—were having an increasingly democratizing effect on the way many churches were run. At the same time, the new high schools and bible colleges were putting considerable pressure on the "lay" traditions of the Mennonite clergy; increasingly, Mennonite ministers were expected to have a good deal of formal theological training. And the steady incursion of the English language

Arnold Dyck, author (GEORGE SAWATSKY)

The famous H. W. Reimer's General Store in Steinbach, Manitoba (CARILLON NEWS ARCHIVES)

Right: *C. T. Loewen, woodworking* (CARILLON NEWS ARCHIVES)

into the Mennonites' daily lives had even breached church life; some congregations were beginning to add sermons in English, or at least were permitting the use of English at Young People's meetings.

Conservative Backlash

So many changes so quickly provoked an understandable conservative backlash, and the 1950s in Ontario and the 1960s in western Canada saw a sharp (if temporary) curbing of the "radicals" in Mennonite churches and institutions. A wave of fundamentalism once again swept through many Mennonite conferences. In Ontario, both Amish and Mennonite churches agonized over issues of "separateness" and over technological innovations; the disagreements produced further splits within several conferences, resulting in the founding of the Conservative Mennonite Church of Ontario. Additional support for this orientation was provided by a steady stream of conservative Old Colony Mennonites returning from Mexico, settling mainly in Manitoba and Ontario. The largely Dutch-German Mennonite Brethren conference actually reversed its policy of ordaining women missionaries and commissioned them instead; more control was exerted over such organizations as the literary societies, which considerably changed them and eventually resulted in their demise. It is probably no coincidence that many Mennonite high schools were closed during this time as well.

Conrad Grebel College, Waterloo, Ontario
(CGC ARCHIVES)

The Founding of the Mennonite Central Committee–Canada

But in 1963 a miracle of sorts, testifying to the undiminished and fundamental charity and peace-making inclinations of the Mennonites (especially when not attempting to sort out theological questions on the congregational floor), occurred with the founding of the Canadian incarnation of the world-famous Mennonite Central Committee. The MCC-Canada is an inter-Mennonite relief and service organization that has incorporated the functions of the many overlapping provincial and regional groups, dealing with such matters as peace education, relief and voluntary service, immigration (sponsorships), government contacts and much else.

The MCC is a dream come true for the many Mennonites who, over the centuries, have despaired over their congregations' tendency to come down repeatedly with the Anabaptist Sickness. Calls for inter-Mennonite co-operation on issues of common concern are almost as old as Mennonitism itself, but a strong tradition of denominationalism has always worked against it. Notable exceptions have occurred, but all proved, in the end, temporary.

At the Brunk Crusade, Rosthern, Saskatchewan, 1955 (CANADIAN MENNONITE ARCHIVES)

Right: *Dockworkers in Calcutta, India, unload Canadian wheat donated by the Mennonite Central Committee—Canada* (AL DOERKSEN/MCC—CANADA)

Family heartbreak: a Holdeman family leaves church after a meeting about the father's excommunication (DAVE JOHNSON PHOTOGRAPH, WINNIPEG/ WESTERN CANADA PICTORIAL INDEX)

Facing page: *A Mennonite family's "consciousness-raising" session: Rev. Erwin Cornelsen and sons.* (ERWIN CORNELSEN)

The MCC works, despite all contrary tendencies, because it is based on the single most unifying element in the Mennonite world: charity. Young and old, conservative or progressive, church Elder or church member, every Mennonite can agree on that. Charity constitutes one of the oldest principles of the Mennonites' Anabaptist tradition. In its name, and at a sufficient remove from the inner politics of the many Mennonite conferences that support it, this organization can undertake projects ranging across the entire spectrum from ultraconservative to radically progressive, with each supporting group seeing largely what it needs or wants to see.

The MCC serves not only Canada but people in need all over the world. It sends relief supplies to dozens of countries every year. It has assisted military draft dodgers from abroad, sponsored war refugees to Canada, petitioned governments against capital punishment, and conducted studies on a wide range of social issues. Its programmes include crime victim/offender reconciliation initiatives, self-help crafts manufacture and sales, Native Indian schools and assistance, and care for the old/infirm/handicapped. Its Mennonite Disaster Service has won grateful acclaim all over North America from the victims of tornadoes, floods and similar disasters, whose houses and farms MDS volunteers have helped to rebuild. And above all, the MCC works in a multitude of ways to oppose war and the military complex ("Make Borscht, Not Bombs").

Mennonite academics at work (CGC ARCHIVES)

Facing page: *Three Mennonite bible school students* (MHC)

The Mennonites Today

With the exception of their most conservative brethren, the Mennonites today can no longer be considered a genuinely "separate" people. Such a separatist tradition was based on the premise of a state hostile to their religious aspirations, and with certain exceptions, Canada's governments have proven generally co-operative. With minority exceptions, most Mennonites today look much like most other middle-class Canadians, and their churches aren't significantly different from those of any other Protestant group. They are no longer a people struggling for survival. The Mennonites have thrived and prospered in Canada, and their numbers are growing vigorously, both within and outside of the church. Their prosperity has been such, in fact, that the stewardship of their wealth has created for them new moral and religious dilemmas.

This does not mean that the Mennonites have set aside their traditional principles of faith, service and discipleship. But with the demise of their separateness, most have set aside some of the older exhortations about involvement with the state and the world. Hardly an election —either provincial or federal—goes by these days without a goodly handful of Mennonites running for political office. Every national political party in Canada has one or more top ad-

visors of Mennonite background. The Mennonites have entered Canada's civil service by the hundreds and even thousands. Mennonite academics teach at almost every sizable university in the country. Mennonites own or have founded some of Canada's largest business enterprises—real estate (Block Brothers), trucking (Reimer's), printing/publishing (D. W. Friesen)—as well as thousands of smaller firms. There are even Mennonite policemen and Mennonite prison guards.

Since the 1960s, another effect of the urbanization of the Mennonites has seen a veritable explosion of artistic creativity among them—particularly in the areas of music, painting and literature. Where the past four centuries had managed to produce only half a dozen serious writers, for example, the past four decades have already produced twice that many (such as Rudy Wiebe and Pat Friesen). Mennonite professional and semiprofessional choirs (such as Winnipeg's Faith and Life Singers and the Mennonite Children's Choir), Mennonite musicians (such as opera singer Ben Heppner) as well as Mennonite artists (such as Gathie Falk) continue to be widely renowned as leaders in their fields.

Fewer than 20 per cent of Canada's approximately 600,000 religious (church members) and ethnic (no longer church members) Mennonites and their children still farm today. Well over half of them now live in cities or suburbs. Canada's cities alone have seen the establishment of between twenty-five and forty new Mennonite congregations (including some Chinese and Asian Mennonite congregations) every decade since the 1950s—although some losses were experienced as well. Shortly after World War II, the Mennonite Brethren in Christ congregations decided to withdraw from the Mennonite family and now call themselves simply the Missionary Church.

The majority of today's Mennonite churches have shifted to the use of English in their services. Pastoral and administrative duties are generally shared among several (paid) ministers rather than concentrated in the hands of the traditional Elder, and ordination tends not to be for life. The election of an Elder, in fact, occurs more and more rarely. Many churches seem to prefer a regular rotation of ministers.

Women have made some gains within the traditionally patriarchal Mennonite world, but not equal to their progress in the secular world. No woman has ever been ordained an Elder, and only a few women serve as ordained ministers. Women serve as missionaries, choir directors, members of church boards and deaconesses (the trend here is toward the election of couples to serve as deacons), but a recent Mennonite Brethren survey showed that only 20 per cent wanted to see more women elected to positions of leadership, and only 5.6 per cent were willing to have women ordained as pastors or ministers. The Swiss-German Mennonites of Ontario have traditionally been slightly more progressive in this regard, but here too, fewer than a dozen women have been ordained as ministers so far, and finding positions for these, despite ready vacancies, has been difficult.

Distinctions: a Reformed Mennonite and a young woman in a minidress, Waterloo, Ontario, 1971 (KITCHENER-WATERLOO RECORD/CGC ARCHIVES)

A women's hospital meeting in a church basement, Manitoba, 1950s (CARILLON NEWS ARCHIVES)

But throughout human history the message has always been greater than the messenger, and throughout their own, the Mennonites have always set themselves rather idealistic standards. In the process of trying to achieve them, they have earned themselves the reputation of an honest, hard-working, God-fearing people, family-oriented, self-sufficient and helpful to their neighbours. As the fifth centennial of their Reformation origins approaches, this is still the case.

From its unique and radical beginnings, the Mennonites' Anabaptist tenets have always provided for a continual redefinition of the church—a series of little Reformations, in effect. The future undoubtedly holds more of these, as a growing fascination with their unusual history leads upcoming generations of young Mennonites to compare the church of their experience with the church of their forefathers' Anabaptist vision—a vision of a believer's church, based on discipleship, the spreading of peace and the uncompromising emulation of Christ. This is the vision—the *special* vision—that may well keep the Mennonite way of life sufficiently "separate" to assure it of a unique future.

The Steinbach Hatchery, 1950s
(CARILLON NEWS ARCHIVES)

Left: *Mixed farming on the East Reserve, Manitoba, 1950s* (CARILLON NEWS ARCHIVES)

Facing page: *Old Order Mennonites harvest grain in rural Waterloo, Ontario* (D. HUNSBERGER/CGC ARCHIVES)

Stock judging, southern Manitoba, circa 1951 (CARILLON NEWS ARCHIVES)

Right: *I. R. Dyck's turkey farm in Manitoba, 1950s* (RED RIVER VALLEY ECHO, ALTONA, MANITOBA)

Facing page: *H. Rempel, Steinbach, Manitoba: modern poultry farming* (CARILLON NEWS ARCHIVES)

Left: *A potato harvest in Steinbach, Manitoba, 1950s* (CARILLON NEWS ARCHIVES)

Right: *A corn harvest in southern Ontario, 1970s* (CANADIAN MENNONITE ARCHIVES)

Marianne Regehr tending sugar beets in Coaldale, Alberta, 1952 (W. AND M. REGEHR)

Right: *Farming near Fort St. John, B.C., 1963* (W. VOLLMAN/NATIONAL FILM BOARD)

Facing page: *Harvesting potatoes in southern Ontario, 1945* (D. HUNSBERGER/CGC ARCHIVES)

Mennonite fruit production, Niagara Peninsula, Ontario, circa 1970 (CGC ARCHIVES)

Left: *Norman Janzen harvests his tomatoes near Plum Coulee, Manitoba, 1955* (RED RIVER VALLEY ECHO, ALTONA, MANITOBA)

The Edward Peters farm near Didsbury, Alberta, 1981 (KATHY PETERS)

Right: *Swathed wheat near Glenlea, Manitoba: John Warkentin and Ernie Wiens assess the results.* (MCC—CANADA)

A typical Mennonite quilting bee, southern Manitoba, 1949 (CARILLON NEWS ARCHIVES)

Left: *Mrs. Friesen and her granddaughter in Steinbach, Manitoba* (WALTER QUIRING)

Facing page: *Johannes Schroeder with his great-grandchildren, Winnipeg, Manitoba, 1957* (W. AND M. REGEHR)

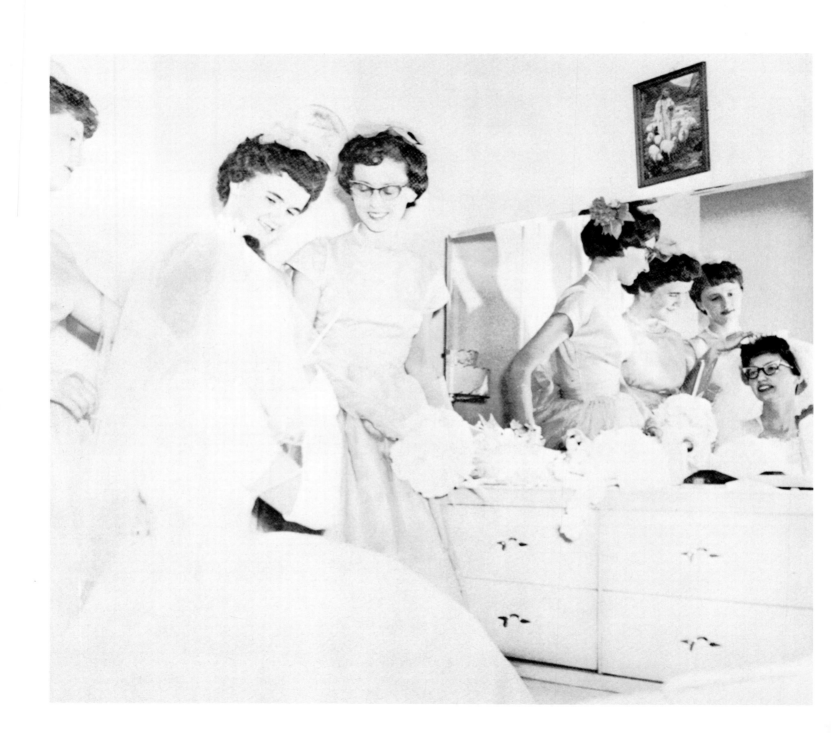

A Mennonite Thanksgiving dinner on the East Reserve, Manitoba, 1950s (CARILLON NEWS ARCHIVES)

Right: *A Mennonite funeral in southern Manitoba, 1950s* (CARILLON NEWS ARCHIVES)

Facing page: *A Mennonite wedding, 1950s style* (WALTER QUIRING)

A Mennonite Festival of the Arts in Manitoba, 1980: making perogies for the Mennonite Pavilion (CARILLON NEWS ARCHIVES)

Right: *A pioneer dinner in Steinbach, Manitoba, 1974* (CARILLON NEWS ARCHIVES)

Facing page: *The Women's Auxiliary at a pioneer dinner* (CARILLON NEWS ARCHIVES)

A golden wedding anniversary (CMBSC ARCHIVES)

Left: *Three generations of Klassens* (AGATHA KLASSEN)

Facing page: *Members of the Bartel clan share a typical Mennonite Sunday dinner, Agassiz, B.C.* (HANNA BARTEL)

Celebrating a seventieth birthday, Prussian Mennonite style (GERTRAUT HOERR)

Facing page: *Teamwork: Rev. Erwin and Hildur Cornelsen preparing a sermon while on holiday, Vancouver, B.C.* (ERWIN CORNELSEN)

Left: *Seniors presenting a programme at the Vancouver Chinese Mennonite Church, Vancouver, B.C.*

Right: *A Sunday service, Mennonite Bicentennial, Kitchener, Ontario, 1986* (D. HUNSBERGER/ CGC ARCHIVES)

An auction sponsored by the Mennonite Central Committee in Morris, Manitoba, to raise funds (MCC—CANADA)

Left: *An MCC native gardening volunteer, Bonnie Cumming, with Aldina Favel and her daughter on the Poundmaker Reserve, Saskatchewan* (BRUCE HILDEBRAND)

Facing page: *An MCC outdoor auction to raise money, New Hamburg, Ontario* (MCC—CANADA)

Mennonite Disaster Service workers to the rescue after the Edmonton tornado, 1988 (BILL THIESSEN, MCC ALBERTA)

Facing page: *Mennonite Disaster Service workers helping to rebuild after a tornado hit LaRiviere, Manitoba, 1968* (CANADIAN MENNONITE ARCHIVES)

Mennonite Brethren Church, Coaldale, Alberta, 1939 (AGNES HUBERT)

Facing page: *The Goodwill Rescue Mission, Guelph, Ontario* (CANADIAN MENNONITE ARCHIVES)

Mennonite church in Steinbach, Manitoba, early 1950s (CARILLON NEWS ARCHIVES)

Facing page: *The Maple View Mennonite (Amish) Church, Ontario, 1964* (CGC ARCHIVES)

Mennonite Brethren Church in Abbotsford, B.C. (CANADIAN MENNONITE ARCHIVES)

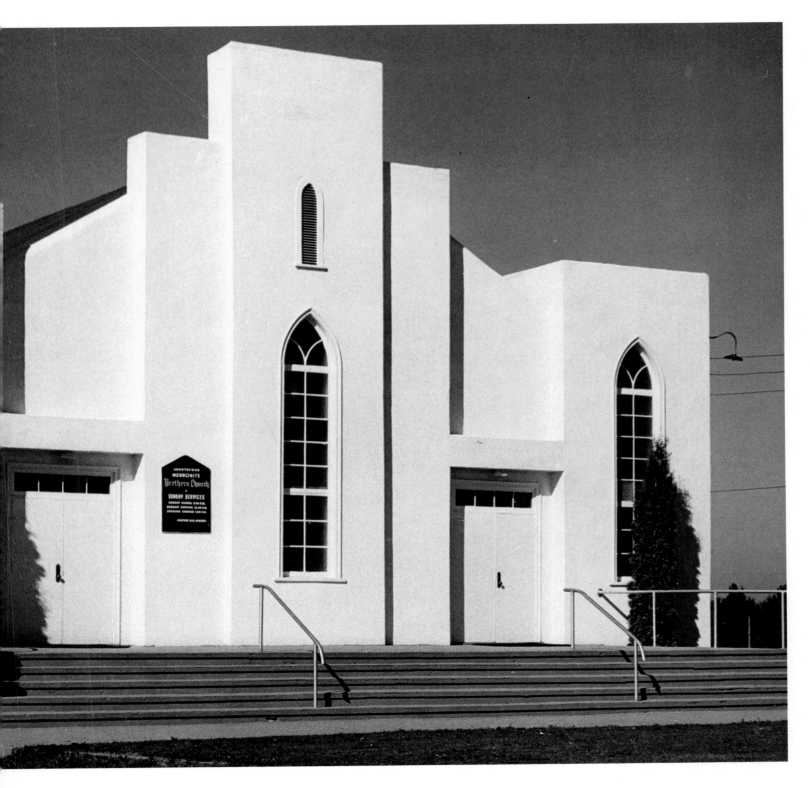

The Steinbach Boys' Band, 1950s
(CARILLON NEWS ARCHIVES)

Reading the Mennonitische Rundschau (CMBSC ARCHIVES)

Facing page: *The master touch: H. Friesen, Yarrow, B.C.* (WALTER QUIRING)

Left: *Paul Hiebert, Mennonite author*
(GEORGE SAWATSKY)

Right: *Junior Choir of St. Jacob's
Mennonite Church, Kitchener, Ontario,
1966* (D. HUNSBERGER/CGC
ARCHIVES)

Top: *Director Rudy Schellenberg exhorts
the Steinbach Bible College Choir, 1980*
(CARILLON NEWS ARCHIVES)

Bottom: *Frank Epp, Mennonite historian*
(CGC ARCHIVES)

Facing page: *Mennonite Children's
Choir, Manitoba, 1971* (CARILLON
NEWS ARCHIVES)

The J. C. Hallman Manufacturing Co., maker of organs, Ontario, 1946 (CGC ARCHIVES)

Facing page: *The Coaldale Cheese Factory, which was in business from 1945 to 1972, Alberta* (JAKE KLASSEN)

Derksen Printers, circa 1946 (CARILLON NEWS ARCHIVES)

Facing page: *C. T Loewen & Sons, southern Manitoba* (CARILLON NEWS ARCHIVES)

PAINTED WITH
Lowe Brothers Paints
SUPPLIED BY
C.T. LOEWEN & SONS

The Loewen Funeral Home, Steinbach, Manitoba, 1950s (CARILLON NEWS ARCHIVES)

Facing page: *D. W. Friesen & Sons Ltd., printers and publishers, Altona, Manitoba* (D. W. FRIESEN & SONS LTD.)

Enns Brothers Ltd., dealers in farm machinery, Winnipeg, Manitoba (ENNS BROTHERS LTD.)

Facing page: *Reimer Express Lines Ltd.* (REIMER EXPRESS)

A Mennonite couple at home in southern Saskatchewan, 1950s (CMBSC ARCHIVES)

Mennonite Faces, Yesterday and Today

Some prominent Mennonite leaders: David Toews (top left), *B. B. Janz* (top right), *S. F. Coffman* (bottom left) *and H. Janzen* (bottom right). (CANADIAN MENNONITE, *top left and top right;* BARBARA COFFMAN, *bottom left;* ERNA WIENS, *bottom right*)

A Mennonite man of yesterday (MHC)

Right: *A Mennonite woman of yesterday*
(CMBSC ARCHIVES)

Two young Mennonite women of the 1950s
(PATRICK FRIESEN)

Facing page: *Johanna Bartel, 1950s*
(GERTRAUT HOERR)

Mr. and Mrs. C. W. Reimer, Steinbach, Manitoba, 1950s (CARILLON NEWS ARCHIVES)

Left: *Prussian Mennonites starting anew in Canada, 1950s: Hans and Hanna Schowalter, Vancouver, B.C.* (H. SCHOWALTER)

Facing page: *Jake Wiebe, a potato farmer near Steinbach, Manitoba, 1950s* (CARILLON NEWS ARCHIVES)

A young Mennonite man of today (MHC)

Right: *Mr. and Mrs. A. L. Reimer, farmers near Steinbach, Manitoba* (CARILLON NEWS ARCHIVES)

Facing page: *Mennonites of yesterday* (CARILLON NEWS ARCHIVES)

A Mennonite married couple (CMBSC ARCHIVES)

Marianne Regehr, starting over in Coaldale, Alberta, 1951 (W. & M. REGEHR)

Facing page: *Three Mennonite farmers tired out after fighting a bush fire near Rosengard, Manitoba, 1948* (CARILLON NEWS ARCHIVES)

A Mennonite man of today (MHC)

Left: *Maynard and Jan Brubacher, 1967*
(CGC ARCHIVES)

Facing page: *Mr. Froese* (GEORGE
SAWATSKY)

A contemporary young Mennonite farmer
(MHC)

Left: *A Mennonite man of today* (MHC)

Facing page: *Old Order Mennonite youths in rural Waterloo, Ontario*
(D. HUNSBERGER/CGC ARCHIVES)

Index

References to photograph captions are in *italic* type.